# THE NEW YORK ATHLETIC CLUB
## Celebrating 150 Years
### 1868-2018

WRITTEN BY NICK VOULGARIS III

New York · Paris · London · Milan

The New York Athletic Club: Celebrating 150 Years is first published in the
United States of America in 2017 by Rizzoli International Publications, Inc., in
collaboration with the New York Athletic Club.

The New York Athletic Club is a private club located at 180 Central Park South
in New York City and at 31 Shore Road in Pelham Manor, New York. In
addition to providing social and athletic opportunities for its members, the
NYAC maintains a steadfast commitment to the support of Olympic athletes
and the spirit of Olympism. Further information about the New York Athletic
Club may be found at www.nyac.org.

Rizzoli International Publications, Inc.
300 Park Avenue South
New York, NY 10010
www.rizzoliusa.com

Publisher: Charles Miers
Text: Nick Voulgaris III
Photography: Bill Abranowicz
Design: Doug Turshen with Steve Turner
Editor: James J. O'Brien
Special Projects Assistant: Richard Koppenaal

ISBN-13: 978-0-8478-6039-5

2017  2018  2019 2020 / 10  9  8  7  6  5  4  3  2  1

Printed in China

Photos courtesy of Getty Images, Victor Sailer/PhotoRun and James J. O'Brien.
Archival photography courtesy of the NYAC archives.

# CONTENTS

# 150TH ANNIVERSARY

When the founders of the New York Athletic Club—John Babcock, Henry E. Buermeyer, and William Curtis—gathered with a clutch of like-minded souls in the Knickerbocker Cottage back in September 1868, could they have imagined the levels of renown that their concept would reach? Indeed, that was all it was back then—a concept. A vague notion of an athletic club, modeled on another, the London Athletic Club, half a world away.

There is no denying that the founding triumvirate had grandiose ideas. As dedicated athletes and competitors, the pursuit of excellence was innate in them. Frustrated with the lack of structure in US athletics at the time, it was second nature to them to get involved and impose structure themselves.

That is not to say that it was easy. It took several failed meetings and plentiful beating of the bushes before sufficient numbers could be spurred to get involved; but great athletes do not know how to give up and, bringing that mentality to the task at hand, Babcock, Buermeyer, and Curtis set wheels in motion, the consequences of which have echoed down a century and a half in ways the world of Olympic sport could never have imagined.

It is important to note, of course, that the founding of the NYAC predates that of the Modern Olympic Games. Certainly, there had been rumblings across Europe relating to a rebirth of the ancient Greek sporting festival; but in 1868, the Olympic Games, as we know them today, were beyond conception. Of far greater import was to build a sporting structure of measurement and competitive opportunity that would allow Americans to excel and to approach the heights of the peerless Britons.

As the ensuing pages reveal, Babcock, Buermeyer, and Curtis quickly piled success upon success and innovation upon innovation. Conditions were often woeful and the path often strewn with obstacles; but, in

1895, when the glorious day arrived that the NYAC went head-to-head with the legendary London Athletic Club in a track and field competition in New York, the success of this fledgling "concept" was keenly evident in the fact that the home team won every event. In Europe, Baron Pierre de Coubertin was marshaling his forces to implement the inaugural Olympic Games of the modern era the following year; but, for the moment, the sporting world could not imagine a clash of athletic titans more significant than this. The New York Athletic Club versus the London Athletic Club? There could be nothing bigger.

If a single event exemplifies what the NYAC was to become, assuredly it is that one. The Club's founders and members set their sights on excellence and then set about defying every barrier that stood in their way. Through commitment, innovation, and an inhuman amount of hard work, those visionary individuals set a precedent that remains hallowed within the NYAC to this day. No organization garners 271 Olympic medals—at the time of publication of this book—without an unwavering commitment to its cause. No organization secures worldwide renown without hewing to its principles with a passion that is resolute. No organization endures for 150 years without clinging ferociously to the tenets on which it was founded, which sustained it through the often stormy seas of its earliest years and which set it on a course for international recognition.

I joined the NYAC as an athletic member of the track and field team in 1978. The pride I took in wearing the winged foot emblem on my vest was enormous. Today, as president of the Club, I am gratified to witness the manner in which the NYAC strives for excellence in every area. At a gala dinner in 2006 celebrating the fiftieth anniversary of his first Olympic gold medal (of four), Club member Al Oerter stated: "Great things are expected of you when you wear the winged foot." These days, we see those words on the reverse of our membership cards. John Babcock, Henry E. Buermeyer, and William Curtis set the wheels in motion; 150 years later, the club that we all enjoy is the manifestation of their vision. As you peruse the following pages, I trust that you will feel a pride comparable to my own in the realization that we all play a crucial part in continuing our peerless tradition.            —*James B. Rafferty, President, New York Athletic Club, December, 2017.*

# INTRODUCTION

It is an honor to have been asked to write the introduction to this very special commemoration of the New York Athletic Club's 150th anniversary.

I have been a proud member of the Club since 1978. My first introduction to the NYAC was via Frank Murphy, a great Irish middle-distance runner who attended Villanova University and who ran for the Club after graduation. Frank would come home to Ireland wearing a gorgeous red NYAC tracksuit. I was a young athlete at the time and I thought that if I was ever lucky enough to get to America, a tracksuit just like that would be a sure sign that I had "made it."

I was lucky enough to make it to America and I was proud to run for Jumbo Elliott at Villanova. After graduation, in 1976 I raced in the AAU Championships at UCLA. I'm the last non-American to have won that race. For some reason, Kenny Schappert and I only had one way tickets to Los Angeles. We had no way of getting back to the East Coast. Ray Lumpp (former Athletic Director) and Jim Rafferty (former Track and Field Chairman, as distinct from the current NYAC president) heard about our problem and were kind enough to take care of it. Soon after, I joined the Club and I've been a proud member ever since.

In the world of Olympic sports, the New York Athletic Club has always been held in the highest regard, predating the shoe companies. In track and field, people such as Ray Lumpp, Jim Rafferty, Tom Quinn, Bob Rodenkirchen, Horace Ashenfelter, and many more ensured that the NYAC was always at the forefront. Jim and Ray became great mentors of mine, and Jim even served as a kind of agent for me over many years. But the NYAC was founded in 1868 in a spirit of amateurism, and that spirit remains to this day, even with the growth of professionalism and corporate sponsorship in the Olympic movement.

The New York Athletic Club has evolved and adapted, maintaining its amateur ethos in the face of competition from the shoe companies, still excelling at the highest levels by presenting "amateur" athletes with the opportunity to compete on the professional stage.

To be a part of all of this is to be a part of the NYAC family. Club administrators, athletes—all Club members—look out for each other, and this network is one of the things that makes the Club very important. Many times, I have traveled the world and met NYAC members who have said, "I saw your photo!" or something similar. There is a lot of pride that comes with being a member of the New York Athletic Club and visitors to the City House and Travers Island are always in awe of what is available.

Personally, I am so proud to have competed for the New York Athletic Club and to remain a member of the Club. The sport of track and field, so essential to the NYAC, has changed enormously over the years, but the NYAC has weathered all of those changes and not only survived, but thrived. It is remarkable to think that, with this book, we are celebrating 150 years of athletic accomplishment. I feel privileged to have played a small part in contributing to the NYAC's celebrated reputation; I know that the coming years will give us even more to celebrate.

—*Eamonn Coghlan, world champion, world record holder, three-time Olympian.*

To my dear friend Geo T. Mitchell, from [illegible]
Year 1887. June 5/30

# CHAPTER I
# HISTORY

# A TRIBUTE TO MY BELOVED NYAC

Being a member of the New York Athletic Club since 1938 has been a pure delight in every way. The Club's facilities in New York City and at Travers Island are perhaps the finest in the nation. The Main Dining Room with the magnificent view of Central Park always makes dinner at our club a very special and memorable event. We are blessed with a superb location.

The greatness of the Club rests primarily on its diverse athletic facilities. At the City House, every sort of athletic facility is available, including an inviting swimming pool and an indoor track. At Travers Island, the Club provides excellent tennis, boating, and swimming facilities, and first-rate dining, especially if you like seafood.

One of my fondest memories is of the warm friendship I developed with the Dufton brothers. Roland Dufton taught me tennis at Travers Island. He was a great teacher but, sadly, I was only a mediocre student and player. However, Syd Dufton, Roland's brother, who was the squash professional at the NYAC, and I became close friends. Syd had been the national professional squash champion, and he was a superb coach who somehow made it possible for me to win the NYAC squash championship for two successive years. Syd was not only a brilliant coach—he later became a very talented biochemical assistant in my laboratory at NYU Langone Medical Center. His companionship and friendship were very wonderful and special to me.

It is such a pleasure for me to express my devotion and appreciation to the New York Athletic Club, which has done so much for so many. Nothing is more important than developing the character and health of our youth, which the NYAC does so well.

*—William Muir Manger, MD, PhD;*
*the NYAC's longest-serving member, having joined in 1938.*

PREVIOUS SPREAD: A rare photo of NYAC athletes with an inscription from renowned swimming and water polo coach Gus Sundstrom. Seated at right is pole vaulter Hugh Baxter. THIS PAGE: Commemorative medals housed in the NYAC Hall of Fame including one from the Amsterdam Olympic Games of 1928.

Wm. B. Curtis.    D.M. Stern.    H.E. Buermeyer.

E. Burris        G.L. Brown              C.H. Cone

# EARLY HISTORY

In the mid-1800s, athletics and formal competitions in the United States had yet to be organized. Instead, amateur sports took place across the country without clearly defined rules or standards for measurements and scoring. Americans interested in track and field or other sports had to navigate fragmented groups and small organizations to compete and pursue their passions.

At this time three men in New York City, William Curtis, Henry E. Buermeyer, and John Babcock, came together to form what would become the New York Athletic Club. They shared an interest in muscle building and competitive athletics.

William Curtis, a sportswriter, was roommates with architect John Babcock in a small apartment at 14th Street and Sixth Avenue in New York City. The men had served in the Civil War and had been acquainted when they both lived in Chicago. They pursued weight training, rowing, and track and field among other sporting endeavors in their spare time. Curtis was known for his speed skating and hammer throwing, while Babcock loved rowing and is credited with inventing the sliding seat for rowing shells.

Through a mutual friend, the two men connected with Henry Buermeyer, who coincidentally also served in the Civil War. He too was extremely passionate about athletics and was the unofficial boxing champion of his regiment in the Union army during the Civil War. As a teen, Buermeyer had won a rowing race around Ellis Island in New York Harbor and had gone on to enjoy success in other sports.

FAR LEFT: Fifty years after its founding, the Club paid tribute to William Curtis, Henry E. Buermeyer, and John Babcock at a celebration at the famed Hotel Astor. LEFT: The first of two photos of four Club members taken twenty years apart. Pictured here in 1884 are (L to R) George Taylor, George Stow, W.G. Morse, and Robert Goffe. The second photo, taken in 1904 and showing the same four gentlemen in clearly robust condition, bore the caption, "A Proof That Athletics Are Not Injurious." It appears on page 45.

With their passion for athletics, the three men converted Curtis and Buermeyer's apartment into a makeshift gymnasium in 1866. They equipped the space with weights, dumbbells, Indian clubs, cables, and other rudimentary equipment needed for their rigorous workouts.

Their goal was to gather likeminded amateur sportsmen at the apartment and create a place to box, swing clubs, and compete in strength training and other sporting activities.

The term "amateur" was key as it was meant to imply no exchange of money. Many individuals involved in athletic competitions in those early days were paid—and often bribed. Following the lead of England's athletic clubs, Curtis, Buermeyer, and Babcock envisioned competitions free of the exchange of money and wagers.

Similar athletic groups that had already formed in England included the London Athletic Club and the Liverpool Athletic Club. These had begun to gain prominence and the three Americans took notice. Realizing there was a rapidly growing interest in athletics in the United States, they wanted to form an organization to propel this movement forward and, more specifically, standardize and record results of the competitions.

Word begin to spread around New York City of the fledgling gym, and athletes interested in competing with one another would come to the apartment and have their abilities measured. The impressive scores of Curtis, Babcock, and Buermeyer were used as a benchmark for the other athletes. The group also organized athletic contests for track and field that quickly became well-attended events. Distances, weights, and times were recorded, which at the time was unheard of in amateur athletics in the United States.

The budding group of athletes began to outgrow the apartment, and the idea of formalizing a club with a proper gym and field began to take shape. The men would

ABOVE: J. Edward Russell, the New York Athletic Club's first president. OPPOSITE: Knickerbocker Cottage, site of the founding of the New York Athletic Club in 1868.

meet at the Knickerbocker Cottage, a small pub nearby at nearby Sixth Avenue and 28th Street, to conceptualize their ideas and plan for a more formalized club.

They realized they would need a decent membership base and money to see the club come to fruition, and they were able to attract interest from rowers at nearby rowing clubs. The three would-be founders began running a series of newspaper advertisements promoting the idea. The newspaper ads yielded interest but no firm responses, and the men were close to giving up. But having persisted throughout 1866 and 1867, in 1868 one final round of advertisements paid off.

There was enough interest to hold a larger public meeting at the Knickerbocker Cottage, and on September 8, 1868, the New York Athletic Club was officially founded. Fourteen men were in attendance, and dues were set at twenty dollars per year, with no initiation fee. J. Edward Russell was elected as the Club's first president. Russell was an excellent athlete, track and field being his foremost activity.

The following day, local New York papers covered the story of the Club's formation and helped garner further interest in the new organization. With the wind in its sails, the NYAC scheduled its first indoor track and field competition for November 11, 1868. The first such competition in United States history, it was held at the nearly completed indoor Empire City Skating Rink, commissioned by the Third Avenue Railroad Company at Lexington Avenue and 63rd Street. Mr. Babcock had been involved with the design and construction of this location, thus giving the Club access.

A staggering two thousand people showed up to watch the event. The New York Athletic Club competed against the Caledonian Club, a social and athletic club for Scottish immigrants.

**Knickerbocker Cottage
6th Ave., 27th & 28th Sts.**

**New York Athletic Club
Organized In This Building
Sept. 8th, 1868.**

# FIRST SEMI-ANNUAL GAMES

OF THE

# NEW YORK ATHLETIC CLUB,

AT THE

## Empire City Skating Rink,

(Third Avenue, 63d and 64th Sts.,)

## WEDNESDAY EVEN'G, NOVEMBER 11, 1868,

At 7 1-2 o'Clock.

---

### OFFICERS OF THE CLUB:

| | |
|---|---|
| PRESIDENT, | J. EDWARD RUSSELL. |
| VICE-PRESIDENT, | J. C. BABCOCK. |
| SECRETARY, | HARRY A. HIERS. |
| TREASURER, | H. E. BUERMEYER. |

---

### COMMITTEE OF MANAGEMENT:

| | |
|---|---|
| WM. B. CURTIS, 200 Sixth Avenue. | CHAS. S. KINGSLEY, 499 Fifth Avenue. |
| H. S. MAGRANE, 90 Chambers Street. | EDWARD FOX, 769 Broadway. |
| DAVID L. G. DORRIAN, 40 Gouverneur Street. | JNO. C. BABCOCK, 200 Sixth Avenue. |
| P. M. BRODERICK, 512 West 42d Street. | H. E. BUERMEYER, 55 Murray Street. |

J. EDWARD RUSSELL. 323 Bleecker Street.

---

### COMMITTEE OF INVESTIGATION:

LT.-COL. WM. E. VAN WYCK.

J. A. GARLAND.         J. O. BALDWIN.

---

*Members will wear the Club Badges.   Managers will be designated by a Blue Rosette.*

LEFT: The program for the first athletic competition organized by the NYAC, an 1868 competition against the Caledonian Club. This was the first indoor track and field competition to be held in the United States. ABOVE: The Empire City Skating Rink, located at 63rd Street and Lexington Avenue, site of the NYAC versus Caledonian Club competition. OPPOSITE: The NYAC was at the forefront of formalizing the rules and regulations of athletic competition in the United States, but the Club was not alone in its passion for sports. The New York Skating Club also boasted an enthusiastic membership base, here pictured on the site of today's Plaza Hotel at Fifth Avenue and Central Park South in Manhattan.

ABOVE: The 1868 competition versus the Caledonian Club also featured the first public viewing of a velocipede, or bicycle, this one imported from France. OPPOSITE: The New York Athletic Club was the first organization in the United States to begin the formal documentation of distances, heights, and times in athletic competitions. Pictured is the original ledger from a competition held at the Club's Mott Haven grounds in July 1874.

For the track portion of the competition, Bill Curtis had sourced a pair of primitive leather running shoes from England that were outfitted with small tacks, or spikes, on the bottoms. This was likely the first time such shoes were used in a properly organized amateur athletic competition in the United States. Another notable event that evening was the first public viewing of a velocipede, or bicycle, which was imported from France and on display.

Although the Caledonian Club performed better on that cold November evening, the event and subsequent press gave the New York Athletic Club substantial publicity. Interest in the Club continued to increase, and membership shot up to one hundred and fifty athletes.

The young club was formally incorporated on April 4, 1870, with ten-dollar shares sold and total capital set at twenty-five thousand dollars. The articles of incorporation were modeled after the London Athletic Club and included language to promote physical culture and encourage outdoor games.

By this point the Club had long outgrown the founders' apartment and had been renting various spaces including a room at a medical college known as Clarendon Hall, a gymnasium on St. Marks Place, and Wood's Gymnasium on Fifth Avenue.

It was at Wood's Gymnasium that a poorly twelve-year-old Theodore Roosevelt would go for strength training as ordered by his doctor. A lifetime of athletics ensued for the nation's future president. He would later become an honorary member of the New York Athletic Club.

For outdoor athletics, the Club had been using Elysian Fields in Hoboken, New Jersey, and Finley's half-mile track at 72nd Street and Broadway. But the lack of permanence presented numerous challenges, and finally the Club leased a small plot of land on the Harlem River near 130th Street. This gave the NYAC not only

## Opening New Club Grounds
### Mott Haven N.Y.
### June 27th 1874

| No | GAME | NAME | CLUB | WINNER | Time |
|---|---|---|---|---|---|
| 1 | 100 yds Handicap | H. E. Quermeyer 3 ft | N.Y.A.C. | H. E. Quermeyer | 11½ |
| 2 | " " | A. H. Curtis 20 " | " " | " " | |

### Second Heat

| | | | | | |
|---|---|---|---|---|---|
| 1 | 100 yds Handicap | W. P. Curtis scratch | N.Y.A.C. | W. P. Curtis | 10¾ |
| 2 | " " | M. E. Curtis " | " " | " " | |

### Third Heat

| | | | | | |
|---|---|---|---|---|---|
| 1 | 100 yds Handicap | W. L. Stow 2¾ ft | N.Y.A.C. | W. L. Stow | 11¼ |
| 2 | " " | A. A. Arnell 13 " | " " | " " | |

### Final Heat

| | | | | | |
|---|---|---|---|---|---|
| 1 | 100 yds Handicap | W. P. Curtis scratch | N.Y.A.C. | W. P. Curtis | 10½ |
| 2 | " " | W. L. Stow 2¾ feet | " " | " " | |
| 3 | " " | H. E. Quermeyer 3 feet | " " | " " | |

### Quarter Mile Run Handicap

| | | | | | |
|---|---|---|---|---|---|
| 1 | Quarter Mile Run | W. E. Sinclair 2 ft | N.Y.A.C. | W. E. Sinclair | 57 sec |
| 2 | " | H. H. Barnes 45 ft | " " | Dead Heat | |
| 2 | " | W. Sprague 45 ft | " " | " " | |

### One Mile Hdcp Walk

| | | | | | |
|---|---|---|---|---|---|
| 1 | 1 mile Hdcp Walk | D. M. Stern 5 seconds | N.Y.A.C. | D. M. Stern | 7.52 |
| 2 | " | E. J. Hudson 46 " | " " | " " | |
| 3 | " | W. A. Bryant 63 " | " " | " " | |
| 4 | " | C. A. McCready 70 " | " " | " " | |
| 5 | " | W. H. Stafford scratch | " " | " " | |

---

## One Mile Walk
### Mott Haven Grounds
### July 11th 1874

**REMARKS**

Prize offered by W. E. Sinclair

E. J. Hudson N.Y.A.C. } Dead Heat Time 8.32
W. E. McCready " " }

---

### Quarter Mile Run
#### Mott Haven Grounds
#### July 11th 1874

Prize club badge offered by Mr. W. E. Sinclair

Waldo Sprague N.Y.A.C. 1    Time 66 sec, won easily
F. J. Haynes " " 2

---

### One Mile Walk
### Match Race
#### Mott Haven Grounds
#### July 13th 1874

W. E. McCready N.Y.A.C. 1 - Scratch    Time 8.30
W. P. Perry " " 21-45 seconds start

---

### One Mile Walk Handicap
#### Mott Haven Grounds
#### July 13th 1874

Y. I. Brown N.Y.A.C. Scratch 1   Time 8.10 (only 2 men finished)
W. E. Sinclair " "   2
E. J. Hudson " "   0
W. E. McCready " 15 seconds 0
C. A. McCready " 45 seconds 0
Y. C. Barnett " 1 Minuet 0
Holbrook New York 1 " 0
Goldsmith " " 1 " 0

LEFT: NYAC athletes with the Club's original trefoil logo. In 1876, the logo was changed to the winged foot design that we know today, seen on the opposite page. The new logo made its first appearance at the inaugural US track and field championships on September 30 of that year. It was designed by well-known architect and champion high jumper Henry Ficken, grandfather of actor Fred Gwynne, best known for his television role as Herman Munster. ABOVE: The sport of fencing was introduced to the United States after a group of NYAC members traveled to Paris in 1878 in order to receive instruction. Pictured is an early NYAC advocate, purportedly B. O'Connor, Jr.

ABOVE, TOP: Local publications were enthusiastic in their coverage of the NYAC's nascent competitions. Impossible to catch on camera, the excitement was imparted effectively by line drawings. ABOVE, BOTTOM: The most important track meets of the 1870s took place at the NYAC's facilities at Mott Haven. RIGHT: Sunday morning exercises at the Club's Mott Haven facility in 1881.

ABOVE, TOP: US President Theodore Roosevelt (R) received boxing instruction from NYAC coach "Professor" Mike Donovan. This illustration was created by Robert Edgren, NYAC member and sportswriter for the *Evening World*. ABOVE, BOTTOM: Rowing was a sport that was embraced from the outset by the NYAC's organizers. Club founder John Babcock is credited with inventing the sliding seat, precursor to the versions globally in use today. OPPOSITE: A gathering of legendary NYAC athletes at Travers Island. Seated (L to R) are Ray Ewry, Harry Lyons, Charles Kirkpatrick, and Mike Sweeney. Standing is Maxie Long.

space in which to build a running track but also access to the Harlem River for rowing. The first track and field meet was held on this site on October 21, 1872.

Colonel William Van Wyck, the Club's second president, was creative in bolstering the Club's finances by renting the advertising rights on the Club's fences to P.T. Barnum and his circus. The Club also rented rooms on Broadway near 35th Street as a temporary clubhouse.

Never an organization to rest on its laurels, in 1874 the NYAC acquired a larger waterfront parcel for athletics farther up the Harlem River between 149th Street and 155th Street. This location replaced the property at 130th Street and would become known as the "Mott Haven Grounds."

A track and field facility was built, as well as a boathouse along the river. The boathouse was two stories, featuring storage for the boats on the lower level and a gymnasium on the second floor. A grandstand for spectators as well as changing houses for the athletes were also erected.

The NYAC prospered in these early days and its membership continued to grow. Having a solid footing, the Club hosted the United States' first national outdoor track and field championships on September 30, 1876. NYAC members won six of the twelve events, and it was there that the Club introduced its winged foot emblem, designed by member Henry Edwards-Ficken and replacing its original "trefoil" logo.

The NYAC continued to be a pioneer in United States' athletics, hosting landmark competitions and, equally as important, keeping records of scores and times. In 1877 the Club organized the first US national championships in swimming along the Harlem River at the Mott Haven property. Swimming pools were rare, so the competition was held in the river and competitors had to deal with cold temperatures, currents, and floating debris. In 1878 the Club hosted the first

**FIRST NEW YORK ATHLETIC CLUB 8-OARED CREW
TO WIN AN OPEN REGATTA
HARLEM RIVER
1888**

PREVIOUS SPREAD, RIGHT: Club rowers on the docks at Mott Haven, along the Harlem River in New York City. Club founder John Babcock invented the sliding seat by creating a device that would move back and forth inside the boat on a rail lubricated with bacon grease. LEFT: The New York Athletic Club lacrosse team in the late 1800s. ABOVE: Robert Rogers, an import from England, was the NYAC's athletic trainer in the 1880s. RIGHT: The NYAC rowing team that won the four-oared shells competition at the Harlem River Regatta in 1883.

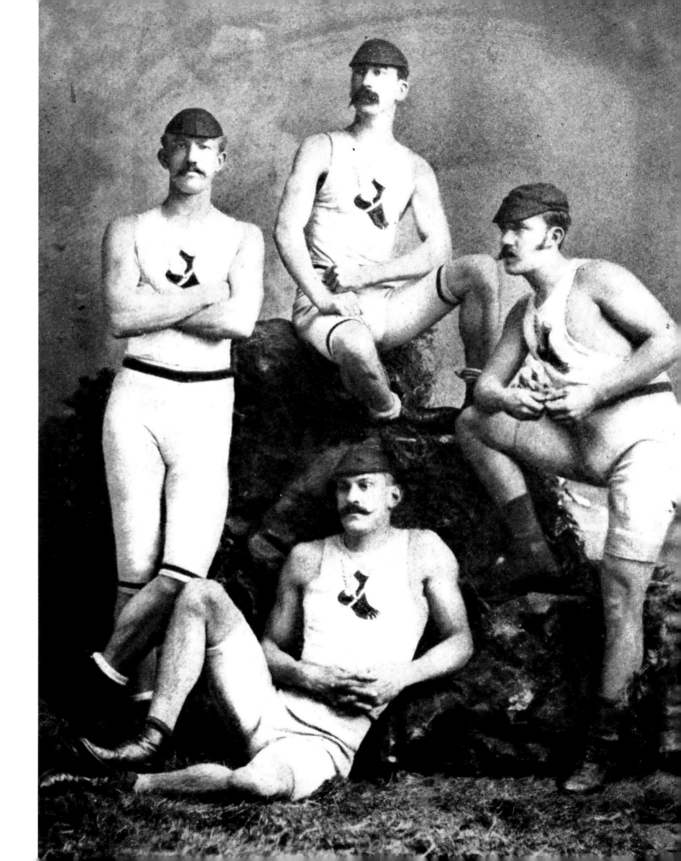

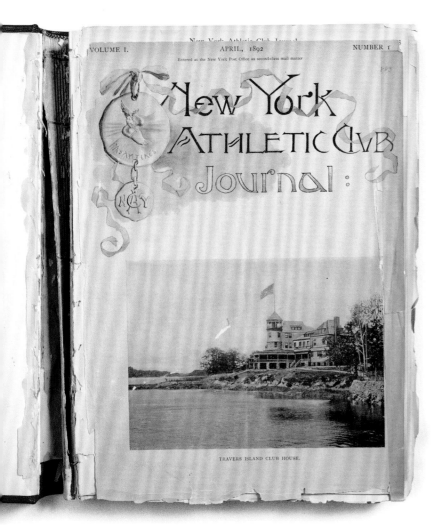

The first edition of the *New York Athletic Club Journal*, published in April 1892. In April 1911, the magazine changed its name to *The Winged Foot*.

national boxing championship at Madison Square Garden, and in 1879, it held the first national wrestling championship.

In 1878 a small group of NYAC members traveled to Paris for fencing instruction, returning to the United States to share this new athletic endeavor with fellow members. Thus the NYAC became one of the first organizations in the United States to introduce fencing as a competitive sport.

Along with athletic clubs from around the country, the NYAC was also instrumental in the founding of the National Association of Amateur Athletes of America (NAAAA) in 1879. The purpose of this organization was to be the neutral governing body to host and manage annual championships throughout the United States, thereby taking the burden off the clubs themselves. In 1888 the NAAAA was replaced by the Amateur Athletic Union (AAU), which had the same mission.

Despite having a growing membership of wealthy individuals, the NYAC's finances were on shaky ground in the early 1880s. This divided the Club into two groups, with one wanting a strictly "no-frills" athletics organization and the other wanting to create a more social club that would have its own clubhouse in Manhattan.

In 1882, financier William R. Travers was elected president; he would oversee the growth and stability of the NYAC's finances as well as its athletic endeavors. Soon after Travers became president, the Club purchased a parcel of land on the corner of Sixth Avenue and 55th Street, the site that would be home to the NYAC's first City House.

A bond was issued to finance the cost of the building, and after several years of construction, the New York Athletic Club's first City House opened in February 1885. This would be the first clubhouse built by a private athletic club in the United States. In strong disagreement with this move, two of the Club's founders, Buer-

LEFT: The Club's first City House at Sixth Avenue and 55th Street in New York City. This was the first purpose-built athletic club in the United States. Note the elevated subway track along Sixth Avenue. ABOVE: William Travers, NYAC president from 1882 to 1887. Travers directed the Club's construction of its first City House, and the purchase of the property in Westchester, New York that was, later, named Travers Island in his honor. A stockbroker and sportsman, Travers was often described as the most popular man in New York. He died in March 1887 from complications of diabetes while convalescing for the winter in Bermuda.

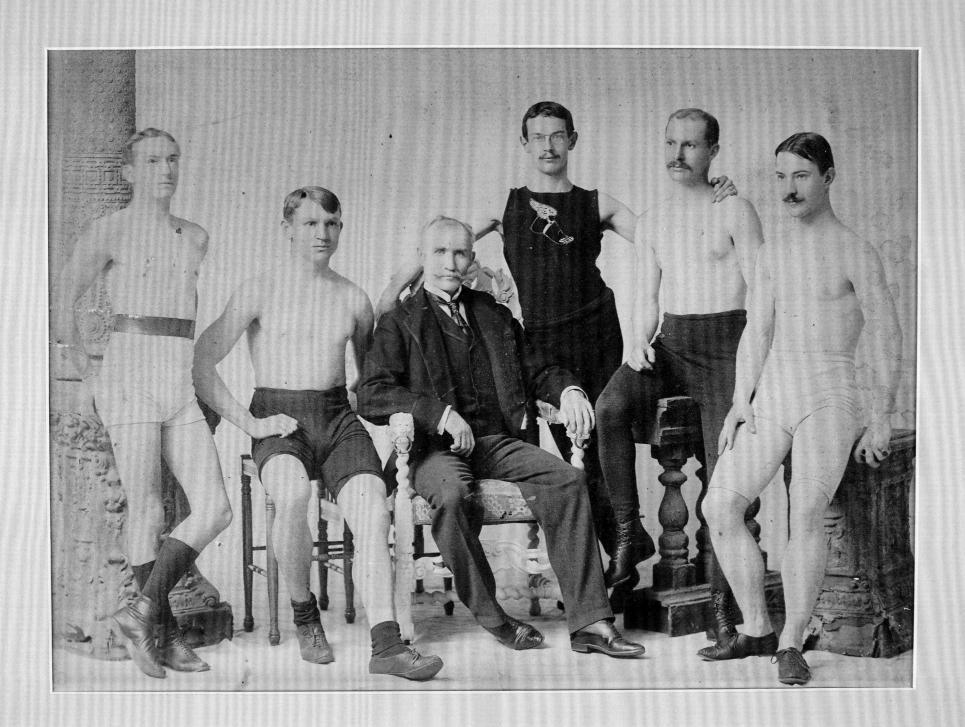

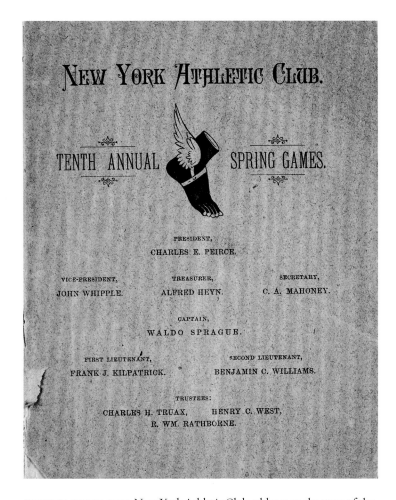

PREVIOUS SPREAD, LEFT: New York Athletic Club athletes on the steps of the Potter House at Travers Island circa 1890. Club President Bartow S. Weeks is seen on the right in the white suit. PREVIOUS SPREAD, RIGHT: Renowned NYAC boxing coach "Professor" Mike Donovan, pictured with Club boxers. ABOVE: A program from the 10th Annual NYAC Spring Games, held at the Mott Haven track at 150th Street in New York City in 1879. The program states Club dues to be twenty-five dollars semi-annually, with a ten-dollar initiation fee. OPPOSITE: The NYAC's Spring Games moved to Travers Island from Mott Haven in 1888, attracting the finest competitors in the nation as well as thousands of spectators. The seeds of the Club's successful rowing program also developed deep roots at Travers Island, and the boathouse was a hive of athletic activity, as it remains today.

meyer and Curtis, resigned; they felt that NYAC funds would be better served supporting athletic programs. Both founders eventually returned as members and were warmly received.

Notwithstanding the trappings of a clubhouse that offered social events, a restaurant, dinners, artwork, and the like, the NYAC rose to the highest echelons of American sport. Top athletic coaches were hired to train its athletes, further securing the Club's preeminent position in athletics. These early coaches included Mike Donovan as boxing instructor, Gus Sundstrom as swimming instructor, Hugh Leonard as wrestling instructor, Mike Murphy as track instructor, and George Goldie as the Club's first Athletic Director.

With membership approaching three thousand, President Travers saw the need to replace the outdoor Mott Haven facility, not just to improve upon it. He successfully pitched the idea of purchasing a sprawling estate in Pelham, New York, to serve as a summer resort for Club members. The property boasted thirty-three waterfront acres, protected waters for rowing, and two large houses. Owned by a business associate of Travers, it was purchased by the Club at the discounted price of sixty thousand dollars on January 14, 1888. A state-of-the-art five-laps-to-the-mile track was installed as well as tennis courts. Yacht racing had become a favorite activity of Club members, and soon the Club erected a separate building with docks to accommodate the needs of members' boats. This facility would ultimately be named Travers Island, in tribute to the man who steered its purchase and development, but who died in 1887 before he could see his vision come to fruition.

The year 1892 marked a milestone in Club history with the publication of the NYAC's own magazine the *New York Athletic Club Journal* (which would eventually become *The Winged Foot* that we know today). The Club's initiation fee was raised to one hundred dollars around this time to cover growing costs.

In 1895, the New York Athletic Club invited the iconic London Athletic Club to an international dual track and field meet. The first international competition of its kind, it was more significant than and helped set the stage for the first Modern Olympic Games, which took place in Athens the following year.

A neutral site was chosen, and on September 21, 1895, the competition was held at the Manhattan Field, a large sporting facility in New York City near 155th Street. The turnout was immense, and the New York Athletic Club enjoyed a total victory, winning all eleven events. This was a highly significant occasion for the New York Athletic Club, cementing its place as the dominant player in international amateur athletics.

While this and other events were taking place, the Club's management realized that the clubhouse they had built just a few years earlier on the corner of Sixth Avenue and 55th Street was inadequate. They had quickly outgrown what had once been an expansive and accommodating building.

Once again the Club raised funds with a bond offering as well as via generous gifts from members including the Vanderbilts, Morgans, Goulds, and Belmonts, and another parcel was purchased, a few blocks north on the corner of Sixth Avenue and 59th Street.

By June 1896, the NYAC had raised close to five hundred thousand dollars toward the building of the new clubhouse. This second City House would have a substantial gymnasium, a swimming pool, billiards room, bowling alley, restaurant, and overnight accommodations. This grand new home was formally opened on March 26, 1898.

RIGHT: In 1895, the New York Athletic Club invited the celebrated London Athletic Club to a dual meet in New York. The NYAC won every event. In terms of global significance, this clash of athletic powerhouses was more significant than the inaugural Modern Olympic Games, held one year later.

OPPOSITE: Charles Kirkpatrick, winner of the half-mile race at the 1895 International Games versus the London Athletic Club.

WHITE. HERBERT. WILLIAMS. JORDAN. OAKLEY. ROBERTSON. SHEARMAN. STEAVENSON. MENDELSON.
BRADLEY. LUTYENS. HORAN. FITZHERBERT.
WILKINS. SHAW. DOWNER.

**THE LONDON ATHLETIC CLUB INTERNATIONAL TEAM.**

At the turn of the century, NYAC membership had risen to more than four thousand, and several Intra Club groups had formed within the Club. The Locusts was a group of elite and powerful members who were involved with the administration of Club affairs. Another club, the Veterans, was founded by Alfred H. Curtis for members who had been active in the Club for at least twenty-five years. Today this group is known as the Quarter Century Club.

Another group, the Huckleberry Indians, was founded by beer magnate Rudy Schaefer, and would meet on a small island that they named Huckleberry Island, located off Travers Island in the Long Island Sound. Schaefer had purchased the island and made it available to the Huckleberry Indians.

Also in 1896, the inaugural Modern Olympic Games was held in Athens. A small group of NYAC athletes made the arduous journey to compete, with Club member Thomas Burke, who also competed for the Boston Athletic Association, winning gold medals in the one-hundred meters and four-hundred meters. The NYAC also sent a contingent to Paris to compete in the 1900 Olympic Games, winning thirteen gold medals, five silver medals, and four bronze medals. At the 1904 Olympics in St. Louis, Missouri, NYAC athletes won seventeen gold medals and thirteen silver medals. With these early successes, the NYAC was on its way to securing a uniquely prominent place within the Olympic movement.

Also in 1904, the NYAC organized the first Block Island sailboat race under the direction of Commodore Henry Jackson. Competing yachts started at Huckleberry Island and headed eastward down the Long Island Sound to finish at Block Island. The roughly 100-nautical-mile race was first won by the yacht *Possum* in sixteen hours. Within a few years, this event became the most important and largest sailing event on the East Coast.

The Huckleberry Indians was founded by beer magnate Rudy Schaefer. They are pictured on Huckleberry Island, their adopted home in the Long Island Sound. The island was named in deference to the free-spiritedness of Mark Twain's Huckleberry Finn. The group also took inspiration from the Native Americans of the Great Plains.

CLOCKWISE FROM UPPER LEFT: NYAC president (1911–12), yachtsman, and International Olympic Committee member Colonel Robert M. Thompson; ten-time Olympic gold medalist Ray Ewry; "The fastest relay team in the world, 1897" (L to R): H.S. Lyons, Thomas Burke, Bernie Wefers, Maxwell Long; Five guests at the Yacht House at Travers Island, 1928 (L-R): Major William Kennelly, Willard Taylor, Sir Thomas Lipton, Sir John T. Walker, Louis Ehret, as Lipton was preparing his fifth and final challenge for the America's Cup; L to R: George Taylor, George Stow, W.G. Morse, and Robert Goffe. Taken in 1904, twenty years after a previous photograph of the same four men, it bore the caption, "A Proof That Athletics Is Not Injurious." The first photo, from 1884, appears on pages 16–17; champion NYAC cyclist Marcus Hurley; the NYAC group aboard the SS Finland, en route to the 1912 Olympics (standing at center is Colonel Thompson along with future Club president William Kennelly, who served from 1926 to 1932, and seated in front of them is Club founder Henry E. Buermeyer).

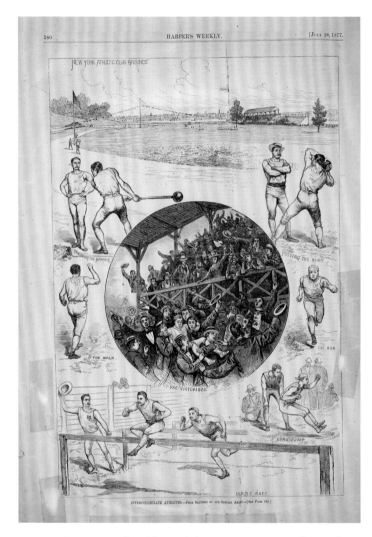

ABOVE: The New York Athletic Club's sporting prowess featured in *Harper's Weekly* in 1877. OPPOSITE: From its earliest days, the NYAC was a wellspring of innovation in the world of athletics. In sprinting in the 1880s, the crouched start was a novel and unproven technique, not universally embraced. The early successes of NYAC athletes such as Charles Sherrill (far right, later captain and manager of the 1900 US Olympic team) and Thomas Burke, winner of the Olympic 100 meters and 400 meters in 1896, helped overcome the early skepticism at such an unusual stance.

Tennis and golf were also becoming popular pastimes for Club members. In 1913 five members, led by Club Governor Louis Bender, provided the funds needed to build the West Side Tennis Club in Forest Hills, New York, which would soon become the definitive destination for tennis competition.

Separately, a group of golfing members lobbied for the Club to purchase a golf course in New York's Westchester County. After much consideration, the Board of Governors decided not to proceed with this endeavor, deeming it to be too much of a financial burden. The golfing group ultimately purchased a course on their own in Mamaroneck, New York, and established Winged Foot Golf Club, named for the NYAC's renowned emblem. The new golf club's first five hundred members were New York Athletic Club members. This organization is, these days, separate from the NYAC, although Winged Foot and the NYAC retain a close relationship, with the Club's annual Athlete's Fund Golf Tournament being held on the celebrated course every August.

World War I was looming, and the NYAC sprang into action to do its fair share in preparation. The Club hired professional soldiers to lead a de facto military training school at the City House. The soldiers would organize regular drills and marches to Travers Island, where the members would train further. Members also raised funds to purchase two ambulances, which, adorned with the winged foot emblem, were sent to France.

Due to the war, most private clubs began to limit their offerings to members by reducing competitions. To the delight of US President Woodrow Wilson, the NYAC bucked this trend by holding weekly athletic events and even sent coaches and athletic gear to US Army and Navy training facilities. The Club was praised for these efforts in the *New York Evening Journal*.

46

ABOVE: Club member and renowned explorer Lincoln Ellsworth flying the NYAC flag on an expedition to the South Pole. OPPOSITE: A 100-meters sprint at the Spring Games at Travers Island, a meet that attracted the finest athletes and crowds approaching three thousand in number.

CONGRATULATIONS
TO THE
N.Y.A.C.
NEWSBOY
ON HIS
50TH ANNIVERSARY

OPPOSITE: Athletic teams of the NYAC: water polo, rowing, hockey, baseball. ABOVE: Celebrated illustrator and NYAC member Robert Ripley commemorated the Club's fiftieth anniversary in his inimitable style.

The military group that had formed at the Club at the start of the war was, ultimately, formally organized as F Company of the 22nd Regiment. Nine hundred and thirty-nine NYAC members enlisted in the armed services during World War I. Additionally, the Club raised millions of dollars to purchase "Liberty loans" and to support organizations such as the Red Cross.

With the signing of the Armistice on November 11, 1918, and the return of peace, members of the New York Athletic Club formed their own post of the American Legion, known as Post 754. Concurrently, the Club was able to return its focus to athletics and NYAC life prospered. However, the introduction of Prohibition in 1920 caused both Travers Island and the City House to suffer financially from the loss of liquor sales.

Reduced revenues notwithstanding, it didn't take long for the Club to realize that, once again, it had outgrown its Manhattan home. In 1926, Major William Kennelly was elected as NYAC president, and one of his goals was to find a new clubhouse. Kennelly's profession was real estate, which helped matters considerably. The Club purchased a large lot on the corner of Seventh Avenue and 59th Street that ran south to 58th Street. The parcel was originally two hundred feet wide, but it was decided to sell half of it, that portion these days being occupied by the Essex House hotel.

Architects York & Sawyer were commissioned to design the new twenty-four-story City House at a cost of roughly $7.25 million. To help underwrite some of the expense, the Club increased the number of members that it would admit from five thousand to six thousand and raised annual dues. Within just a few years, membership would rise to an impressive eight thousand.

New York Athletic Club Site
59th St. and 7th Ave.
York & Sawyer, Architects
Charles T. Wills, Inc., Builders
Made Oct. 21, 1927

Irving Underhill
NYC

B50 634

OPPOSITE AND RIGHT: Construction of the Club's third, and current, City House got underway on the corner of Seventh Avenue and Central Park South. The site had been previously occupied by New York City's first co-operative apartment complex, the Spanish Flats. ABOVE: (L to R) Past NYAC Vice-President Alfred H. Curtis, NYAC President Graeme Hammond, former President Bartow S. Weeks, and founder Henry E. Buermeyer standing at the site of the Club's founding at Knickerbocker Cottage, located on Sixth Avenue between 27th and 28th Streets.

The New York Athletic Club's City House at Seventh Avenue and Central Park South opened in 1929. Its many amenities included an expansive barber's shop.

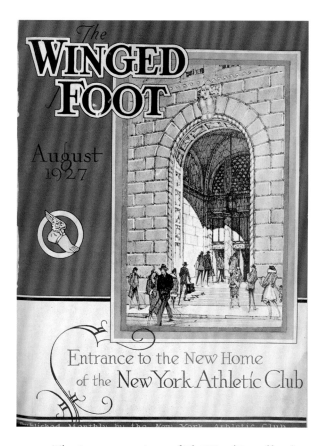

ABOVE: The August, 1927 issue of *The Winged Foot* offered a foretaste of the Club's third City House that was to open less than two years later. RIGHT: Famed illustrator, explorer, and NYAC member Robert Ripley of *Ripley's Believe It or Not* was also an avid handball player. Ripley paid for the addition of handball courts on the roof of the City House at 59th Street and Sixth Avenue.

The stock market crash of 1929 at first had little effect on the finances of the NYAC, but the devastating consequences inexorably rolled in. By 1932, there had been an exodus of members who had lost much of their wealth, and membership dropped from eight thousand to a startling two thousand.

Austerity measures were put into place, which included closing several floors of the City House to save on utilities and staffing. Rates for rooms and dining were dropped to help attract weary patrons. Employees took pay cuts, and services were minimized. William Kennelly, the Club's president, proposed that a group of members who were still sufficiently affluent purchase the Club and save it from bankruptcy. This idea wasn't widely accepted, and, in 1933, Kennelly resigned and William Dalton was elected as the new president.

Dalton set out to reorganize the Club's finances and to restructure and defer mortgage payments as allowed by the bankruptcy laws put into place as a result of the crash. He is credited with saving the Club from complete financial ruin. Creative perks were initiated at the City House and Travers Island in order to lure new members. The City House held live performances and Broadway-type shows as well as the first of a long tradition of All Sports Dinners. At Travers Island, women's changing rooms were installed, a pioneering move at the time for a private men's club.

Although the Club had tremendous debt and was struggling to make mortgage payments, athletics was still a focus. Trapshooting, golf, boxing, track and field, swimming, water polo, and other sports pushed forward despite the bleak economic conditions. The well-attended Saturday Morning Boys Program was a welcome refuge for sons of members.

ABOVE: New York Athletic Club swimmers Walter, Wallace, and Leonard Spence, featured in a 1935 issue of *Vanity Fair*.

ABOVE: The NYAC powerhouse water polo team with later-to-be NYAC president William "The Eagle" McCarthy standing second from left. OPPOSITE: Olympic hopefuls: the 1936 NYAC crew included Jack Sulger, patriarch of the Sulger rowing dynasty, and Jim Parker, later to become general manager of the New York Athletic Club. That year's competition for Olympic Games selection was immortalized in the best-selling book *The Boys in the Boat.*

The Club's baseball team won close to 90 percent of the games it entered in 1934, while members continued to thrive in many other sports and bring further recognition to the New York Athletic Club. A young Peter Fick became the world swimming champion at one-hundred-yards freestyle, and the noted Spence brothers—Wallace, Walter, and Leonard—also won accolades in swimming. Water polo, handball, and fencing joined the spotlight with numerous victories and national titles. NYAC rowers shone in 1934, with John Ryan winning the national senior singles title.

In 1935, several members who were interested in fishing formed the NYAC Angler's Intra Club. And in 1936, despite the challenging economic road ahead, the Club still managed to allocate sixty thousand dollars toward athletics to keep the Club's mission alive. This post-Depression era saw an influx of new members and, thankfully, the membership base began to expand once again.

The NYAC sent athletes to compete in the 1936 Olympics in Berlin, despite the AAU's concern over the rise of Adolf Hitler and fear that he would use the event for propaganda. The athletes sailed to Berlin on the SS *Manhattan* with NYAC representatives in track and field, swimming, rowing, water polo, and fencing.

For the remainder of the decade, the Club continued to enjoy victories in many sports including water polo, tennis, swimming, wrestling, and basketball. In addition, softball was introduced to the Club for the first time.

The Japanese attack on Pearl Harbor in 1941 drastically changed the political and social landscape as the country entered the Second World War. Once again, members stepped up to support the war effort with money and personnel. Both the City House and Travers Island were offered to the government for use and an enormous amount of sporting equipment was donated to aid in military training.

J. Sulger    F. Silvio    J. O'Sullivan    H. Sharkey    A. Walz    J. Rodgers    D. Scannell    J. Parker

J. Dominick

N.Y.A.C. Olympic Contender Crew ~ 1936 ~ Lake Carnegie, Princeton, N.J.

Travers Island became the home of the Norwegian navy, which used the property as a base of operations for training as well as lodging. A ceremony took place at which the NYAC flag was formally lowered and both the Norwegian and American flags were raised. A number of the private yachts that were berthed at Travers Island were relinquished to the US Navy and Coast Guard for service, many operated by NYAC members.

Throughout the Club's history, over two thousand members have served in the armed forces; forty-three have given their lives. In the 1940s members raised a staggering $30 million by purchasing war bonds to help in the war effort. The Club also created a special Armed Services Membership that offered reduced fees to those members serving in the military. The Club's American Legion post offered numerous services for the veterans, including job placement, entertainment, athletic programs for children, and financial support for families of veterans killed in the line of duty.

The year 1943 marked the seventy-fifth anniversary of the founding of the Club. A gala event took place in the gymnasium of the City House on November 10, with more than twelve hundred members present. The turnout was illustrative of the NYAC's capacity to rebound after the Depression and war. And in spite of the war, the Club kept its focus on athletics, winning dozens of national and metropolitan championships in 1943 and 1944.

By 1946, life began to return to normal at the New York Athletic Club. With the war over, the government returned Travers Island to the Club, and a formal NYAC flag raising took place on May 16 of that year.

The Club still faced tough economic challenges as a result of the 1935 financial reorganization. There was a first mortgage of close to $4.5 million

ABOVE: During World War II, Travers Island was commissioned for use by the US military, which offered the facilities on loan to the Norwegian navy. At a special ceremony, the NYAC flag was lowered and the US and Norwegian flags were raised to fly together.
OPPOSITE: Norwegian sailors departing Travers Island in 1945.

ALL SPORTS DINNER
N.Y.A.C.

April 20, 1932.

EMPIRE
photographers
N.Y.

that was due to mature in 1955 and a second mortgage of close to $1 million that also had to be addressed. Travers Island was in need of costly upgrades and repairs after its years of wartime use. The Club began to solicit summer members for Travers Island, with the additional revenue used to make upgrades to the property.

The challenges were somewhat eased by the addition of five hundred new members and as food and room rentals once again became a good source of income. President Frank Sieverman wanted each department within the Club to be self-supporting—this way allowing revenues to be directed toward athletics.

The Club flourished once again, and by 1948 its indoor track and field meet at Madison Square Garden, with sponsorship by the Ford Motor Company, was broadcast on network television to an estimated half-million viewers.

Different challenges and strong public criticism lay ahead, however. In 1968 Professor Harry Edwards from California's San José State College accused the NYAC and the US Olympic Committee of racism. In a speech, the professor blasted the Club for being exclusionary and pointed the finger at the Olympic movement for only having a few "token" minorities competing in the Games.

Edwards orchestrated a boycott of the Club's 1968 Indoor Games at Madison Square Garden. The event, intended to be a celebration of the one hundredth anniversary of the Club, was instead the center of a highly charged protest with threats of violence. The meet took place without significant incident, but the protests called for the Club to choose between retaining its private status and continuing its public role in sponsoring its annual track and field meet. The

OPPOSITE: First held in 1932, the NYAC All Sports Dinners remain a social highlight of the Club's calendar. In the early days, a boxing ring was set up in the middle of the room allowing members to enjoy the bouts while dining. Today's Beefsteak and Boxing events in the City House harken to those earlier years. ABOVE: Having weathered depression, war, and financial strife, the Club cleared the mortgage on the present City House in 1968. Board members presided over a ceremonial burning of the document.

NEW YORK
ATHLETIC
CLUB

100th
ANNIVERSARY
1868 – 1968

INDOOR GAMES
MADISON SQUARE GARDEN
FEBRUARY 16, 1968

OFFICIAL PROGRAM                    ONE DOLLAR

ABOVE: The NYAC Games held in Madison Square Garden were comparable in status to the legendary Millrose Games track and field meet. In 1968, a time of considerable social strife, the NYAC meet was subject to boycott, meaning that the one hundredth edition of the NYAC Games was also the last. OPPOSITE: As members exit the City House onto Central Park South, they do so via revolving doors beneath an oft-overlooked gem, a golden clock that is stunning in its intricacy. Beneath it is the gilded visage of Neptune.

decision was taken to remain private and reluctantly the curtain came down on the NYAC Games.

Ironically, the Club's efforts in promoting athletics for all races during this period were never recognized. The NYAC, in fact, helped subsidize an African-American athletics club by paying its dues in the AAU for ten years and paid for the group's travel around the country to compete in national championships.

Another wave of social change affected the fabric of the New York Athletic Club; during the 1980s, due to the efforts of the national women's rights movement, women were allowed to become members of private clubs from which they had hitherto been excluded by virtue of gender. Up until that point most private clubs had restrictive membership policies that were exclusionary. The New York Athletic Club adopted an open policy towards women and minorities and both groups were quickly embraced.

In the decades since the City House mortgage was finally paid off (accompanied by a celebratory burning of the mortgage document), the Club has enjoyed an expansion to more than nine thousand members and continues to be the predominant athletic club in the United States, if not the world. The New York Athletic Club has been designated as the foremost athletic club in the United States by the Club Leaders Forum and continues to invest tremendous resources in the support of Olympic athletes and those who aspire to be. The following chapters showcase the significance of the NYAC in the world of international athletics as well as within the cultural fabric of New York City.

# CHAPTER II
# CLUB HOUSES

# OUR ICONIC HOMES

I remember my first reaction, in 1962, on approaching the New York Athletic Club City House from West 59th Street and visually absorbing the west and north façades. Being a young architect, it was natural for me to delight in experiencing the entry procession. From 59th Street, one proceeds through the articulated arched groin vault leading into the elegance of the Lobby. I became a member that year, enjoying the many amenities offered at the NYAC.

The present City House was designed by the architectural firm of York & Sawyer, completed in 1929 in the Renaissance Revival style, an example of the classicism of the Beaux-Arts popular at the time. The site was originally occupied by the Spanish Flats co-operatives. The co-operatives experienced mortgage difficulties and, in 1928, the site was purchased by the Club. The instruction given York & Sawyer was for a multistory building with many different uses. The resulting floor-by-floor assignment of the interior functions was well conceived and is evident in the final design.

One can summarize four major groupings: athletics and aquatics on floors three to eight; entertainment on floors nine through twelve; overnight guest rooms on floors fourteen through twenty; and a roof deck / solarium overlooking Central Park. Being a multipurpose building presented opportunities for architectural exterior expressions, vis-à-vis the Loggia on the Seventh Avenue façade providing exterior access to the ninth-floor Lounge and Card Room. On the north façade are the accentuated ninth-floor windows, as well as the classic pediments of the eleventh-floor Main Dining Room windows. Similarly creative fenestration can be observed on the façade of the gymnasium and Aquatics Center.

It was of great interest to me, in 1962, to learn of Travers Island. In 1888, the Club purchased some thirty-three acres of land in the Pelham–New Rochelle area on the Long Island Sound, a "club away from the Club" with all the amenities of a country club. In June of 1889, the first Travers Island Club House was built, subsequently replaced by the elegant TI Club House of today. My wedding reception and that of my daughter were held at the Club and hold a special place in my heart, all being part of a gratifying journey of membership in the NYAC.

—Anthony Di Santo, former NYAC Board member and noted architect

19 27

THE · NEW · YORK · ATHLETIC · CLUB · oF · THE · CITY · OF · NEW · YORK · ORGANIZED · 1868 ·

Central Park South     NEW YORK ATHLETIC CLUB     New York City

# THE CITY HOUSE

The NYAC's first City House (far left) was purpose built for the Club and erected on the southwest corner of 55th Street and Sixth Avenue. The formal opening took place on February 5, 1885, and was covered by the *New York Times*. The Club opened its second City House in 1898 and the third—and current—(left) in 1929.

Thanks to the innovative thinking of the founders and early officers of the New York Athletic Club, members are today fortunate to enjoy two very impressive clubhouses, one in Manhattan and one in Pelham Manor, New York. While they differ in terms of character and amenities, they share the Club's mission of promoting athletics and providing elite social and recreational opportunities for members.

The New York Athletic Club was the first organization of its kind to maintain both a city and a country clubhouse, largely due to the efforts of William Travers, who was Club president from 1882 to 1887.

As outlined in the previous chapter, in 1885 the New York Athletic Club opened its first City House, located at Sixth Avenue and 55th Street in New York City, an initiative that Travers pioneered. He emphasized the need to attract new members, thereby bolstering the Club's finances and generating funds that helped to underwrite the construction of the new clubhouse. It was a dramatic change from the humble apartment that the Club's founders used at Sixth Avenue and 14th Street, back in 1868.

The 55th Street City House was not only a great new facility for members—it also proved to be a shrewd financial investment. The Club quickly outgrew that building, the proceeds from its sale helping to finance a larger home a few blocks north at Sixth Avenue and 59th Street.

The 59th Street location, purchased in 1892 and opened in 1898, included expanded gymnasium facilities, overnight accommodations, and a swimming pool. But as with the first clubhouse, the Club's rapid growth was too much for the building to accommodate. Once again, proceeds from the sale of the property were used to help finance the purchase of a new site, one that would become the Club's current home on the corner of Seventh Avenue and 59th Street.

This site had originally been the location of New York City's first co-operative apartments, known as the Spanish Flats. The Club's president at the time, Major William Kennelly, had seen the need for a new building. A real estate professional, in 1923 he began negotiating the purchase of the property and in 1926 he secured the deal. The parcel was on the corner of Seventh Avenue, running from 58th Street to 59th Street extending two hundred feet to the east.

The architectural firm York & Sawyer was commissioned to design the Club's new home, with construction and property costs at about $7.25 million. Half of the site was ultimately sold and now accommodates the Essex House hotel.

The lavish new City House was to feature an impressive gymnasium and track, a swimming pool, nearly two hundred overnight guest rooms, a restaurant, a tavern, and a ballroom. Construction began soon after the Spanish Flats building was razed, and a formal cornerstone-laying ceremony was held in November 1927. In attendance were over fifteen hundred people including New York City mayor Jimmy Walker, Club officers, Club members, and other dignitaries. The NYAC's third City House opened for members' inspection on December 25, 1928, with a formal opening on January 22, 1929. This new building would be the Club's ninth city location and one of the best-equipped athletic facilities in the

ABOVE: Located on the northeast corner of Seventh Avenue and Central Park South, the Spanish Flats was the first co-operative apartment complex in New York City. The NYAC purchased the site for the construction of the third City House, which opened in 1929.
OPPOSITE: The second City House was built on the eastern corner of Sixth Avenue and Central Park South. (Note the elevated subway tracks.) Partly financed by August Belmont, with other benefactors including Goulds, Morgans, and Vanderbilts, it opened in 1898 and stayed in use until the opening of the current City House in 1929.

012684 NEW YORK ATHLETIC CLUB, NEW YORK          COPR. DETROIT PHOTOGRAPHIC CO.

The laying of the third City House's cornerstone in 1927. Many city dignitaries were in attendance, including Mayor Jimmy Walker (pictured above right front corner of the stone) and Major William Kennelly, NYAC president from 1926 to 1932 (with striped tie).

world. The City House remains one of the most iconic buildings on Central Park South, its rooftop views extending to the northernmost reaches of Central Park at 110th Street and, on a clear day, considerably beyond.

This newest City House was built with a grand double-height lobby embellished by a golden statue of Mercury that, to this day, holds pride of place. The athletic facilities are vast, accommodating countless sports. The Aquatics Center on the third floor features a twenty-five yard swimming pool, plus a steam room, sauna, and hot tubs. The gymnasium on the sixth floor features an elevated

74

Members and guests entering the Lobby of the current City House are inevitably awed by its elegance. Pride of place among artifacts is the statue of *Mercury and Caduceus.* Cast in Italy, it is believed to be one of only two in the world. Fashioned in the style of Giambologna (1529–1608), it was presented to the Club in 1898 by Charles T. Wills, whose company was awarded the general contract to build the present City House. Mercury's winged feet inspired member Henry Ficken to create the celebrated emblem that now denotes the New York Athletic Club around the world.

The City House Lobby immortalizes its most celebrated athletes—who received the Veteran's Trophy for Athletic Progress—as well as those members who served and lost their lives in World War II, Korea, Vietnam, and the attacks of 9/11.

TAXI CABS

ABOVE: The Hall of Presidents on the ninth floor houses striking portraits of many Club presidents. OPPOSITE: The City House Solarium, formerly a members' lounge, later housed yoga, judo, and a golf net. Most recently, it is a popular rooftop tapas bar.

running track, a full-sized basketball court, and first-class weight-lifting and cardio training equipment.

On the seventh floor are a judo facility, two boxing rings and five squash courts. The twenty-first floor features courts for racquetball, doubles squash, and handball. The basement, which at one time boasted a bowling alley, now has training facilities for wrestling and fencing.

The City House features an elegant Main Dining Room on the eleventh floor with singularly beautiful views of Central Park. For a more casual social setting, the popular Tap Room, is styled after an English pub with a large, welcoming bar and dining area. On the ninth floor, the Library boasts leaded-glass cabinetry containing volumes of historic literature, bound issues of *The Winged Foot* dating from 1892, and current publications and best-sellers.

For overnight guests, the City House has one hundred and eighty-seven guest rooms and suites. There are also numerous conference rooms and banquet halls for functions of all kinds, from small business meetings to the most elegant of weddings. The American Legion Post of the New York Athletic Club, founded in 1919, is still active in its home on the twelfth floor.

The Club's Hall of Fame and Hall of Champions on the second floor house a collection of awards that highlight 150 years of athletic accomplishment, most particularly at the Olympic Games. It is in this room that the mission of the Club's founders—to promote amateur athletics—is most clearly manifest.

The City House is a beautifully functioning facility with over three hundred full-time employees who attend to the every need of members and guests. The spirit of collegiality for which the NYAC is renowned is made all the more so by its staff, many of whom have been in the Club's employ for more than twenty-five years.

PRECEDING SPREAD AND RIGHT: The intricate design of the ceilings in the ninth-floor Lounge illustrate many of the Club's traditional sports. With its ornate fireplace and mantel, the room is popular for all manner of gatherings, from chess and backgammon to business meetings and weddings. The views of Central Park and the works of art make it all the more appealing. FAR RIGHT: A portrait of legendary NYAC fencer Arthur S. Lyon, a three-time Olympian, captain of the US Olympic fencing team in 1924, and one of only two men to qualify for the US Olympic team in all three weapons.

86

The ninth-floor Card Room, adjacent to the Lounge, exudes the calm and charm associated with card and board games. The ornate ceilings replicate face cards.

The walls of the Card Room immortalize the NYAC's champions through the years.

TO THE ETERNAL MEMORY OF

| JAMES S. BEECHER | EDWARD F. DORGAN | LOUIS J. LEDERLE, Jr. |
| WAYLES B. BRADLEY, Jr. | ARTHUR L. ENGELS | CHARLES O. MAAS |
| JOHN R. BUCKINGHAM | DANFORTH B. FERGUSON | JAMES A. McKENNA, Jr. |
| HERBERT A. BUERMEYER | HENRY D. GILL | JOHN PURROY MITCHEL |
| HERBERT A. COLLINS | H. NORMAN GRIEB | ARTHUR MYERS |
| ROBERT A. CRANE | RICHARD D. HAMILTON, Jr. | JOHN W. OVERTON |
| | MARSHALL G. PEABODY | CHARLES W. STEWART |

Formerly the Trophy Room, these days the second floor of the City House is home to the NYAC Hall of Fame. Among the ornate artifacts are the Lipton Trophy (above) presented to the NYAC by tea magnate Sir Thomas Lipton and which was awarded annually to the winner of a one hundred-mile race from Huckleberry Island to Block Island, and the intricate James H. Hughes Memorial Trophy (right) which was presented to winners of a four-and-a-half-mile race across the Long Island Sound.

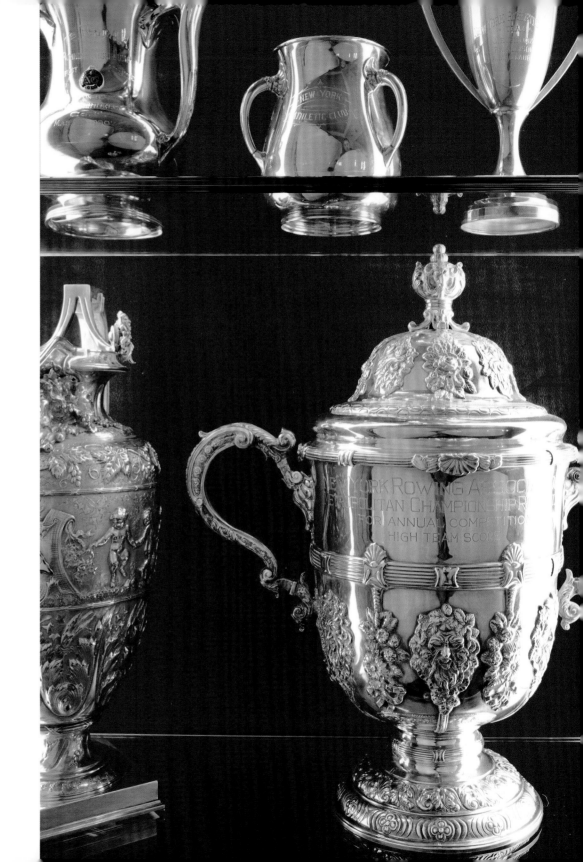

Billiards.

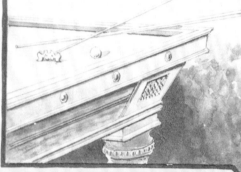

·· BOWLING ··

As they always have, interviews for membership take place on the ninth floor. An interview can, these days, be followed by a cocktail at the ornate and welcoming bar adjacent to the Main Dining Room on the eleventh floor. The views of Central Park are entrancing.

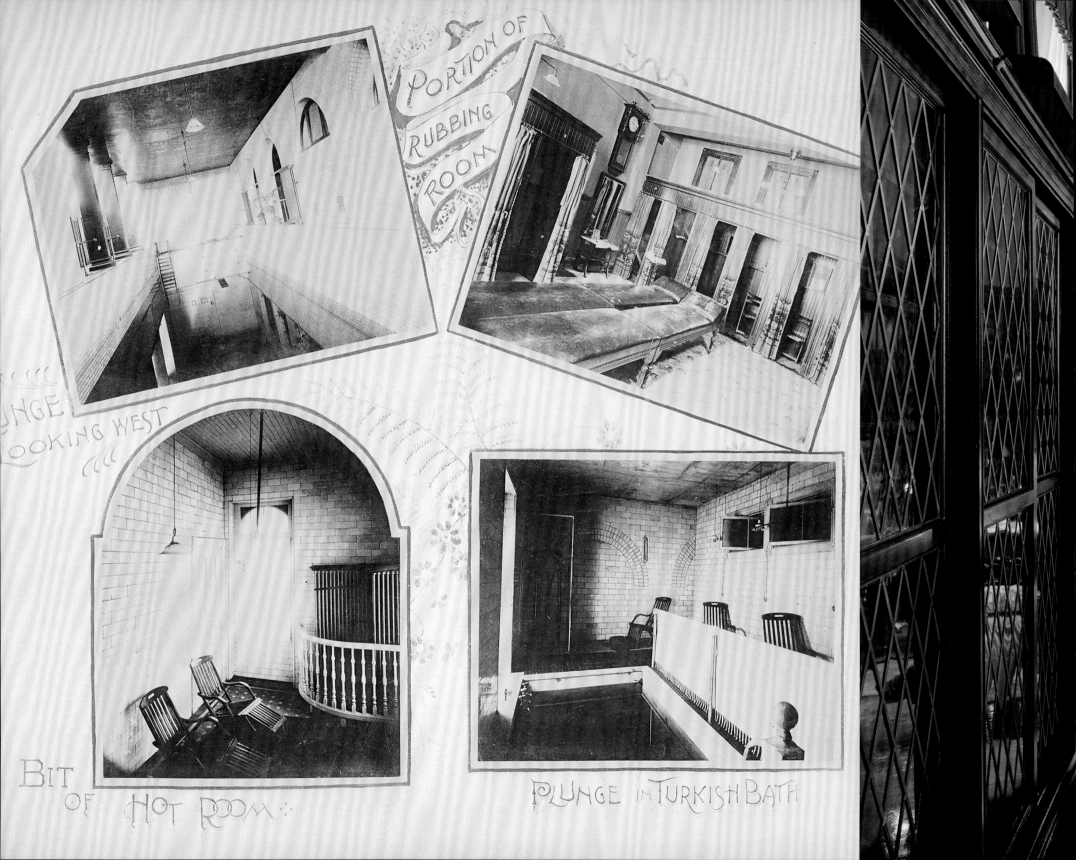

PORTION OF RUBBING ROOM

LUNGE LOOKING WEST

BIT OF HOT ROOM

PLUNGE IN TURKISH BATH

Club founder William B. Curtis was reputed to be "America's Greatest Amateur Athlete." That spirit of athletic excellence endures in the expansive sixth-floor gymnasium, as it does in the third-floor Aquatics Center (following pages).

WATER POLO TEAM

# TRAVERS ISLAND

ABOVE: In the years before the NYAC acquired its own purpose-built facilities in the City House and at Travers Island, Club athletes swam and rowed at Mott Haven, located between 149th and 155th Streets along the Harlem River. OPPOSITE: Prior to the installation of the saltwater pool at Travers Island, the area between the Club House and the Long Island Sound featured a beautifully sculptured garden with a sundial.

During his tenure as president in the late 1880s, William Travers recognized that the NYAC was outgrowing the Mott Haven property along the Harlem River. Travers felt that the Club needed a proper country home that could accommodate more track and field competitions, more rowing boats, and a wider range of outdoor sporting activities.

A committee was formed to find a suitable location in reasonable proximity to the City House. Hog Island, a twelve-acre island in Pelham owned by the family of Club member Arthur Hunter, was identified. The property also included four acres on the mainland and a stone causeway that connected the two parcels. On January 14, 1888, the Club purchased the land for sixty thousand dollars, which also included the rights to fill in approximately sixteen acres of surrounding water and mud flats, bringing the total acreage to more than thirty. William Travers died before the close of the sale of the island, and in his memory the NYAC renamed the property Travers Island.

The property was heavily wooded and contained large rocks and boulders left by glaciers, typical of the northern shores of the Long Island Sound. At the time of its purchase, the property contained two dwellings. The first was a large residence near the north end of the island known as the Hunter House, which was used as a temporary clubhouse while a new one was being built on the property. The other building, known as the Potter House, served as a training facility. Because of its rough terrain, substantial excavation, drilling, and filling were needed to make the property usable for athletic purposes; however, with that completed, the

waterfront property quickly became an ideal and idyllic location for track and field competitions, rowing, swimming, yachting, and trapshooting.

Almost immediately after purchasing the property, Athletic Director George Goldie oversaw the construction of the Club's first tennis courts, thus introducing a new sport to members. Goldie also oversaw the installation of a state-of-the-art five-laps-to-the-mile running track that allowed the Club to host national championships. A baseball field was also constructed in order to accommodate what was becoming an increasingly popular sport.

After the tennis courts and athletic field were built, the construction of a boathouse followed later that same year. The boathouse was a two-story structure that featured storage and launch facilities for the rowing craft, docks, lockers, and a training room.

Travers Island soon became a popular second home for Club members, and in the warmer months it wasn't uncommon for them to ride their bikes from the City House to their new Westchester retreat. Such early grumblings as existed at the purchase of so remote a property were quickly dispelled as members enjoyed the new athletic campus and the opportunity to be outdoors and close to nature.

The New York Athletic Club's new clubhouse at Travers Island officially opened in 1889. Just prior to the opening, the Hunter House, which had served as a temporary clubhouse, was ravaged by fire. Fortunately there were no injuries—the rowing crew that had been housed there narrowly escaped, thanks to a warning from their barking dog.

The new clubhouse was an imposing three-story wooden structure that resembled a Norman château. It was lavish, with a piazza surrounding the main floor that had sweeping views of the Sound. It also included a restaurant and bar, parlors, reception rooms, and overnight accommodations for seventy-five guests.

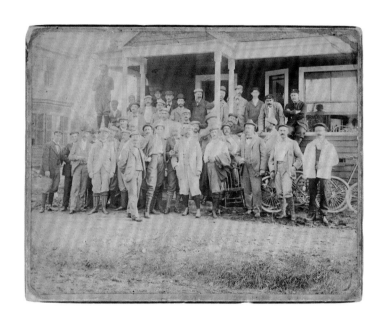

OPPOSITE: The interior of the Club House at Travers Island. ABOVE: Club members gather on the steps of the Potter House at Travers Island.

The new building even had hot and cold running water in its bathrooms, a rarity at the time. An impressive wine cellar was constructed and stocked with the finest wines and champagnes.

In 1901 this new clubhouse would also be lost to fire. Further upsetting was that the building had housed William "Buffalo Bill" Cody's collection of cowboy and American Indian memorabilia, all of which was destroyed. The famous Wild West entertainer had donated these items to the Club years earlier. With the loss of the clubhouse, the Potter House was called into action and used as a temporary home until plans were made for the construction of a new facility.

In 1892 the NYAC built a yacht house with a float and pier to cater to the Club's growing fleet of member-owned yachts and steamboats. A few years later a second yacht house was constructed to accompany the first. As sailing interest grew, the Club began to organize yacht races in Long Island Sound.

In keeping with the Club's mission to promote and support amateur athletics, NYAC sportsmen were encouraged to live at the island in order to avoid distractions, to avail of the facilities, to benefit from teamwork, and to maximize the effectiveness of their training regimens.

The Club's Spring and Fall Games, held at the Mott Haven grounds since 1869, continued at Travers Island, quickly attracting thousands of spectators who arrived on special trains from New York City and surrounding areas. Soon bicycle racing became a popular sport, while football, lacrosse, trapshooting, fencing, ice skating, and the aforementioned baseball also were introduced. Trapshooting became so popular that the first-ever national championships were held at Travers Island and continued there for many years.

U.S. Olympic Champions

R.S. Barbuti 1928    R.W. Landon 1920    J. Anderson 1932    H. Hillman 1904

T.I. 1933

Paul Pilgrim 1906    H.J. Babcock 1912    R. Ewry 1900-4-6-8    J. Jones 1904    M. Long 1900    M. Adams 1912

Travers Island

After Travers Island's experience with fires, the new clubhouse, erected in 1908, made use of fire-resistant materials of brick and concrete. The building was constructed on the site of the Potter House, which had been removed, and was finished with a white stucco façade and red tiled roof. It contained similar accommodations to the previous clubhouse but also boasted a three-thousand-square-foot dining room, substantial commercial kitchen space, and fifty-five private sleeping rooms. Travers Island even had its own power plant for electricity, with coal brought in by barge to power the generator. The Travers Island Club House of today, substantially renovated in 2002, stands on the same site as its 1908 predecessor.

In those early days, the boathouse and waterfront activities at Travers Island quickly grew to be significant parts of the property's activities. Yachting and sailboat racing became a favorite competitive sport, and yachtsman and tea magnate Sir Thomas Lipton donated the "Lipton Trophy" to the Club in 1912. The trophy was awarded annually to the winner of the one-hundred mile race from Huckleberry Island to Block Island. Today this trophy can be seen in City House's Hall of Fame.

The entrance of the United States into World War I on April 6, 1917, spurred Club member and Broadway composer George M. Cohan, just one day later, to write the iconic "Over There" still one of the best-known wartime show tunes. Cohan wrote several other patriotic songs including "The Yankee Doodle Boy" and "You're a Grand Old Flag." It is believed that Cohan presented the first public performance of "Over There" at Travers Island before a battalion of members who were volunteering for service. Travers Island would continue to serve as a training facility throughout World War I.

The enhancements made through the years at Travers Island would be put to use during World War II by the US government. A partnership with Norway saw Travers Island and all of its amenities turned over to the Norwegian navy in

Composer, bandleader, and Club member George M. Cohan wrote numerous Broadway standards, including "The Yankee Doodle Boy," "You're a Grand Old Flag," and "Over There," the latter wartime show tune making its debut at Travers Island.

1943, symbolized by a formal lowering of the NYAC flag and a raising of the US and Norwegian flags. Norwegian troops trained for battle and lived at the facility, and yachts stationed there were used to patrol the Long Island Sound. For many years, a portrait of the queen of Norway hung over the mantel in the Travers Island clubhouse, a reminder of the Club's support of the war effort.

There have been many modifications to the Travers Island amenities over the years. In addition to the main clubhouse, the yacht club, tennis house, and boathouse, there is a saltwater swimming pool that is used both for recreation and competition. More recently, construction was completed on a field house, fully staffed with top-class trainers, that contains a wide of array of fitness and training equipment. Travers Island also runs a comprehensive summer program and day camp that engage children in a range of sporting opportunities including sailing, track and field, swimming, and tennis.

Today Travers Island is a beautifully maintained facility and a spectacular asset for members of the New York Athletic Club and their guests. It provides a sanctuary beyond the hustle and bustle of New York City where members can connect with nature, fresh air, and the water, just as they have since 1888.

Visitors to Travers Island are invariably overwhelmed by the beauty and tranquility of the property and the manner in which those elements are complemented by the broad array of events, activities and facilities. As it has since its purchase, Travers Island—like the City House—furthers the Club's mission of fostering amateur athletics while also offering social, recreational, and dining amenities that are second to none.

Situated on thirty-three idyllic acres alongside the Long Island Sound, the always welcoming Club House at Travers Island offers dining amenities with views that are second to none.

With the US and Club flags surveying the action, the all-weather athletic field at Travers Island sees year-round first-class competition in rugby, lacrosse, and soccer. The field is situated where once the nation's foremost running track was located.

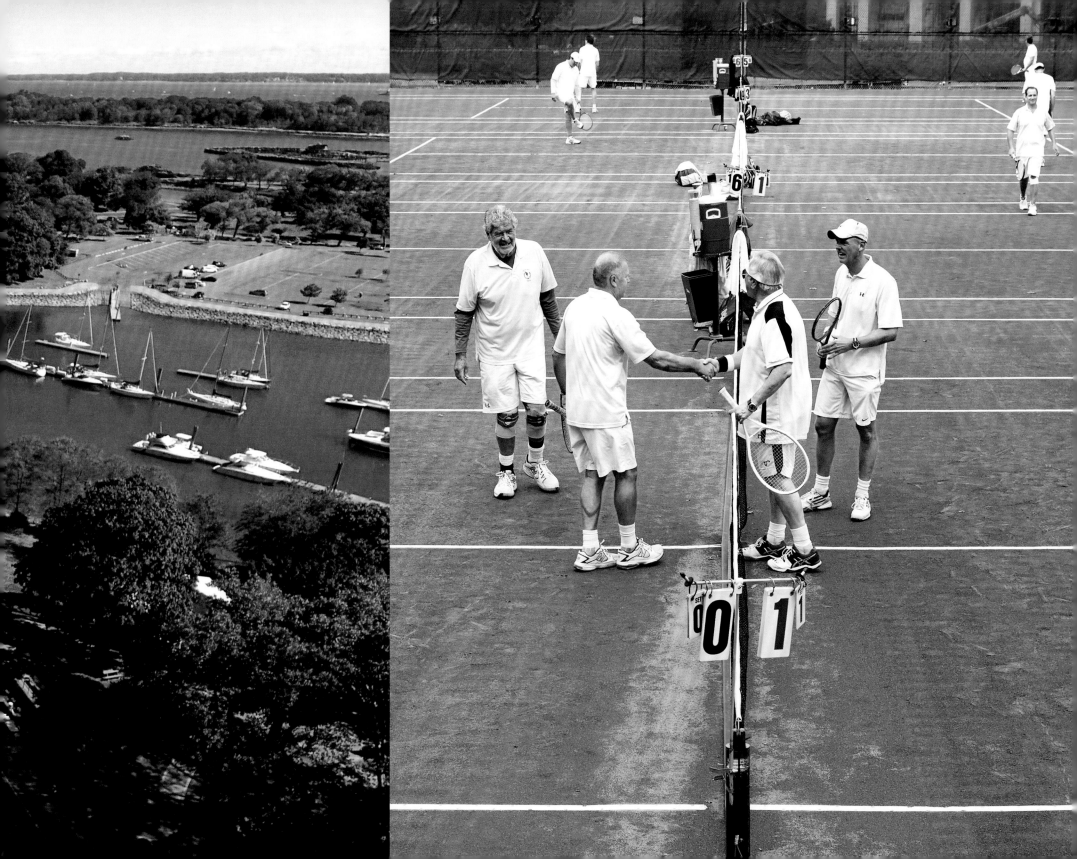

TWENTY-FIRST ANNUAL FALL GAMES
TRAVERS ISLAND
SEPT. 22ᵈ 1888

# CHAPTER III
# OLYMPIC GAMES

# A SPECIAL PLACE FOR OLYMPIANS

The New York Athletic Club is a special place for Olympic athletes. In the late 1970s, when I was a high school wrestler in New Jersey, I would always hear about the great NYAC wrestling tradition, and I dreamed of being able to compete for the Club. As I developed into a quality wrestler in college, Sonny Greenhalgh, the Wrestling Chairman, asked me to compete for the NYAC. This was an awesome offer; I was going to wear the prestigious winged foot on my singlet.

In 1984, when I won the gold medal in heavyweight freestyle wrestling at the Los Angeles Olympic Games, I became an Olympic member of the Club. Before I was done, I won four Olympic medals, two golds (1984 and 1992), one silver (1988), and one bronze (1996), plus nine World Championships medals: three golds, three silvers, and three bronzes, all while representing the New York Athletic Club. I competed my entire senior career as a proud member of the NYAC.

One of the truly unique events at the Club is the All Sports Dinner, held each fall honoring that year's NYAC elite athletes. This is where I met one of my Olympic heroes, Al Oerter, who became a very good friend before his passing in 2007. Al was a four-time Olympic champion, winning the discus competition in 1956, 1960, 1964, and 1968, setting Olympic records each time. He represented the NYAC in his four Olympics and was a lifetime Club member. Al had a great perspective on life, was an NYAC Hall of Fame member, and had a true respect for the Club. The All Sports Dinner continues to bring together great athletes and is an annual celebration of elite athletics at the NYAC.

The NYAC is a unique organization and remains one of the most important athletic clubs in the Olympic movement. The tradition of Olympic medalists and team members is second to none. Without a doubt, the NYAC was instrumental in my success as an Olympic wrestler as it has been in the successes of countless athletes over the Club's 150-year history.

The New York Athletic Club is well respected in the US Olympic movement and throughout the world. I can emphatically say that the NYAC is a true champion of the Olympic spirit. —*Bruce Baumgartner, four-time Olympic medalist*

Patrick McDonald   R. Craig   Harry S. B...

Charles D. Redpath   J E ...

Platt ...   ... W. Kelly

...ke P Kahanamoku   Ralph W Rose   ...

...ott McGrath.   James Thorpe   A W Richards   Albert ... Gutterson

July 26th 1912 — To Warren from Ann

# OLYMPIC GAMES

PRECEDING PAGE: The flag, signed by US team members, including Jim Thorpe, that was flown on the SS *Finland* that transported the Olympic team to Stockholm for the 1912 Olympic Games. The flag presently resides in the NYAC Hall of Fame. OPPOSITE: Members of the 1908 US Olympic team. Standing (L to R): Forest Smithson, Harry Hillman, John Flanagan, Ralph Rose, John B. Taylor, Nathaniel Cartmell, and Ray Ewry. Back row seated (L to R): J. B. Maccabe, Gustavus Kirby, Bartow S. Weeks, James E. Sullivan, John Hayes, Mike Murphy, Matt Halpin. Second row seated (L to R): Lawson Robertson, John Garels, Charles Daniels, Martin Sheridan, Mel Sheppard, Edward Cook. Front three (L to R): Frank Irons, unknown, Charles Bacon.

The New York Athletic Club has a long and rich history of involvement in the Olympic Games. Indeed, Pierre de Frédy, Baron de Coubertin, universally acknowledged as the founder of the Modern Olympic Games, became a member of the Club during a visit in 1893. The founders of the NYAC had a passionate interest in sporting contests, having been inspired by British organizations such as the London Athletic Club, at the time the world's preeminent track and field club. Prior to the commencement of the Modern Olympic Games in 1896, the New York Athletic Club invited the London Athletic Club to an international dual meet in the United States. The first event of its kind, this clash of titans took place in New York City on September 21, 1895. The NYAC beat the British club in all eleven events. In athletic terms, it was a competition—and a result—of global significance, more important than the nascent Olympic Games, set to take place the following year in Athens. In no uncertain terms, it established the New York Athletic Club as an international athletic powerhouse.

De Coubertin, along with Prince George of Greece and William Sloane from the United States, had a broader vision, however, and advocated for a competition that tested the talents and strengths of athletes from around the globe in a variety of sports. The men began to cement the idea of a large-scale international gala open to countries from around the world. The beginnings of the Modern Olympic Games were humble, but the concept soon began to attract attention from all corners of the world.

New York Athletic Club member Thomas Burke, who also competed for the

Boston Athletic Association, won the one-hundred meters and four-hundred meters at those first Games. After Burke's great win, the New York Athletic Club was moved to increase its participation in the Olympic Games in subsequent years. A larger contingent was sent to Paris in 1900 including NYAC legends Ray Ewry, Maxey Long, I. K. Baxter, Alvin Kraenzlein, and George Orton. Charles Sherrill led the group as captain and team manager. The group won twenty-two medals: thirteen golds, five silvers, and four bronzes. Ray Ewry would go on to be the Club's most decorated Olympian, as well as one of the most decorated Olympians of all time. Competing in the now discontinued standing jumps, he would claim ten gold medals in four different Olympic Games.

At the 1904 Olympic Games in St. Louis, NYAC athletes won an astonishing fifty-two medals: thirty-two golds, nine silvers, and eleven bronzes. By this time, the New York Athletic Club had secured its position of prominence in the world of global athletic competition and as a dominant player in the Olympic movement.

Athlete and Club member Matt Halpin served as manager of the US Olympic team for the 1906 Inter-Calated Olympic Games in Athens, Greece. The NYAC team won five gold medals and one silver. Halpin played a significant role within the athletics administration of the New York Athletic Club and also served as captain and team manager of the US team at the 1908 Games in London, where the NYAC team won six golds, three silvers, and three bronze medals. There likely would have been many more medals won that year, but the US team suffered misfortune while voyaging across the ocean—six athletes were severely injured when the ship transporting them, the SS *Barbosa*, was slammed by an unusually large "rogue" wave.

By 1912, interest in the Olympics was continuing to grow but it was still unclear if the new concept of an international games would survive. Many New York Athletic Club members stepped forward to lend their financial support to further

THIS PAGE, CLOCKWISE FROM TOP LEFT: Harry Hillman, 1904 Olympic gold medalist, 400 meters, 200-meters hurdles, 400-meters hurdles; the NYAC team for the 1895 International Games versus the London Athletic Club; Maxwell Long, 1900 Olympic gold medalist, 400 meters; Charles Bacon (R), 1908 Olympic gold medalist, 400-meters hurdles. OPPOSITE: Paul Pilgrim, winner of the 400 meters and 800 meters at the Inter-Calated Olympic Games of 1906 in Athens. Following the disorganization of the St. Louis Games in 1904, the 1906 Games were hastily formulated in order to reinvigorate a movement that was in jeopardy. Pilgrim later became Athletic Director of the NYAC.

the Club's presence and success at the Games. NYAC president Colonel Robert Thompson initiated contributions to the Olympic Fund, along with fellow members J.P. Morgan and Andrew Carnegie. Thompson was also president of the American Olympic Committee—later to become the US Olympic Committee—and a leading force in supporting the Games and working for their success.

In order to ensure that the athletes had proper food and accommodations for the 1912 Games, held in Stockholm, Sweden, Thompson chartered the 560-foot ocean liner SS *Finland* to transport the US Olympic team across the ocean and back. The lavish ship, equipped with comfortable sleeping cabins and a team of chefs, also served as the athletes' hotel while in Stockholm. To accommodate the athletes and their training needs during the voyage, the ship was modified to include a one hundred-yard cork track for sprinting, while a fifteen-foot-by-five-foot canvas pool was built on the deck for swimming. Bikes were secured on the deck so that cyclists could stay in shape.

In the early morning hours of April 15, 1912, less than one month before the Stockholm Games began, the RMS *Titanic* struck an iceberg in the North Atlantic and sank with the loss of more than fifteen hundred lives. Four New York Athletic Club members were aboard; two perished from exposure from the icy water. Naturally there was much trepidation about making the transatlantic voyage on the SS *Finland*. But after the ship's integrity was confirmed and the number of lifeboats deemed more than adequate, the trip ensued. The Club's Olympic team performed excellently in Stockholm, and the dockside hotel proved to be a great asset. The team won thirteen gold, four silver, and two bronze medals.

The American Olympic team bound for the Paris Olympic Games of 1900 comprised largely of athletes from the NYAC and the University of Pennsylvania. Back row, L to R: J.W.B. Tewksbury, John Bray, George Orton, Lew Sheldon, Alvin Kraenzlein, Alex Grant, Irving K. Baxter, Unknown. Center row, seated, L to R: Walter Carroll, Joseph McCracken, Bascom Johnson, Ray Ewry, Charles Sherrill, Bob Garrett, Richard Sheldon, John Flanagan, Michael Murphy. Front row, seated, L to R: Dixon Boardman, Arthur Newton, Maxwell Long.

By the conclusion of the 1912 Olympics, it was clear that the Games conceived by de Coubertin would endure. It was decided by the International Olympic Committee that the 1916 Olympic Games would be held in Berlin, Germany. A large new stadium would be built under the supervision of the German Olympic Committee.

The outbreak of World War I in 1914 forced the cancellation of the 1916 Games. New York Athletic Club members Theodore Roosevelt and Ambassador James Gerard led a rally to encourage members to enlist in the military and to support American allies. Athletes of the New York Athletic Club were some of the fittest in the country, and their physical condition proved very useful as they entered basic training.

Perhaps the efforts and sacrifices of amateur athletes during the war influenced public opinion, because by the war's end, sports, training, and fitness were even more widely recognized and supported than hitherto in the United States and around the world. This helped the growth of the New York Athletic Club and increased global interest in the Olympic Games.

The Games resumed in 1920 and were held in Antwerp, Belgium. This was a challenging time for the Olympic movement after the devastation and chaos of World War I. But despite financial and logistical challenges, the Belgians staged a successful event. The New York Athletic Club sent a delegation of thirty-two athletes to represent the United States. Pat McDonald, who enjoyed many successful competitions at Travers Island, won a gold medal in the fifty-six-pound weight throw, setting a new world record. In total the NYAC won nine gold, two silver, and four bronze medals.

On December 11, 1911, NYAC President Robert M. Thompson, also president of the American Olympic Committee and a member of the International Olympic Committee, hosted a dinner at the City House for members of the AOC. The event looked forward to the Stockholm Olympic Games, set to take place the following year and at which the NYAC hoped to excel. In the center of the table is a model of the Stockholm Olympic Stadium, complete with the flags of each nation expected to compete.

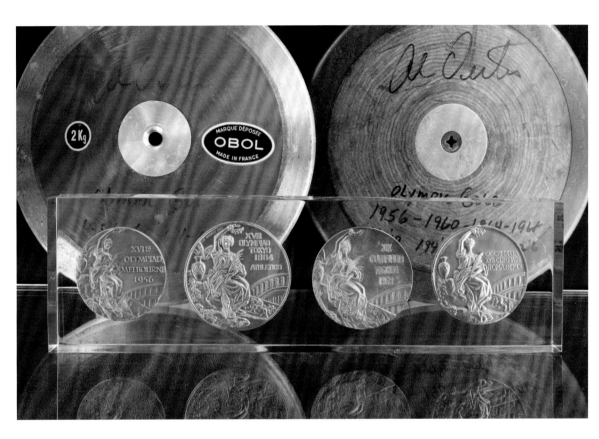

PRECEDING SPREAD (LEFT), CLOCKWISE FROM TOP LEFT: Jackson Scholz, 1920 4x100-meters relay Olympic gold medalist, 1924 200 meters Olympic gold and 100 meters silver medalist; Harry Babcock, 1912 pole vault Olympic gold medalist; Richmond Landon, 1920 high jump Olympic gold medalist; Lindy Remigino (center) claims the Olympic gold medal in the 1952 100m. PRECEDING SPREAD (RIGHT): The Hall of Champions on the second floor of the City House acknowledges the Club's deep and enduring association with the Olympic Games. OPPOSITE AND ABOVE: In the annals of the Olympic Games, there are few more celebrated names than that of NYAC member Al Oerter. At the Games of 1956, 1960, 1964, and 1968 Oerter won the discus throw, having entered the competition as an underdog on each occasion due to, by his own admission, inexperience, injury, or age. Asked to explain his success, he coined the immortal phrase, "These are the Olympics, and you die for them." Oerter also stated, "Great things are expected of you when you wear the winged foot." Today that motto appears on the reverse of every NYAC membership card. Disci signed by Oerter are housed in the NYAC Hall of Fame, as are replicas of his medals.

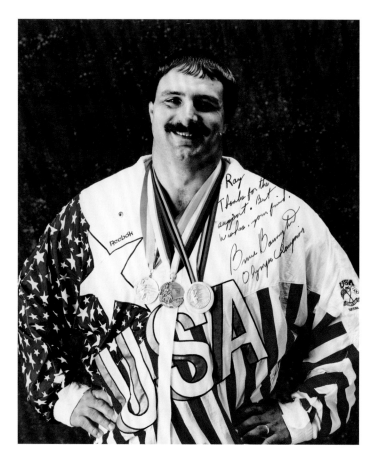

ABOVE: Bruce Baumgartner is unquestionably one of the greatest wrestlers in Olympic history, having won gold medals in 1984 and 1992, a silver medal in 1988, and a bronze medal in 1996. He also won nine world championships medals, three of each color.
OPPOSITE: At the 2008 Olympic Games in Beijing, Team USA, with six NYAC players in the squad, secured silver medals. Pictured L to R: Rick Merlo, Adam Wright, Tony Azevedo, Merrill Moses, Layne Beaubien, and Jesse Smith.

In 1924, Colonel Thompson, still the head of the American Olympic Committee, once again stepped forward to organize the New York Athletic Club's participation in the Olympic Games, these held in Paris. He organized another ocean-going vessel to transport the athletes and rented a lavish château outside of Paris for the team and guests. The 1924 Olympics are immortalized in the 1981 film *Chariots of Fire*, with Club member Jackson Scholz, who won a gold medal in the two-hundred meters and a silver in the one-hundred meters, portrayed in several scenes.

Games founder Pierre de Coubertin, who to this point had retained his title as head of the International Olympic Committee, formally stepped down after the 1924 Olympics. It was only fitting that the final Games over which he would preside were in his home country. He was succeeded by Count Henri de Baillet-Latour.

In the 1928 Olympic Games in Amsterdam, the New York Athletic Club was represented by sixteen athletes. The team won six gold medals and one each of bronze and silver. The medals were claimed in track and field, swimming, and wrestling.

These early Olympic Games were the foundation of the NYAC's longstanding involvement in competitions of the highest level all around the world. Global competition has evolved tremendously since the Club's first international meet in 1895, when the London Athletic Club was invited to a clash of athletic giants in New York City.

In each subsequent Olympics, the New York Athletic Club has not only been a participant but a dominant force. Men and women representing the NYAC have competed in sports including track and field, rowing, tennis, water polo, fencing, swimming, judo, table tennis, trapshooting, and wrestling, to name a handful, bringing home literally hundreds of medals. Some of those athletes have been among the most celebrated in Olympic history.

Discus thrower Al Oerter became the first track and field athlete to claim gold medals at four consecutive Games, these coming in Melbourne in 1956, Rome in 1960, Tokyo in 1964, and Mexico City in 1968. Kayla Harrison became the first American—male or female—ever to win a gold medal in judo, taking the crown in London in 2012. Against the odds, Harrison repeated that feat in Rio de Janeiro in 2016. In the sport of wrestling, Bruce Baumgartner proved himself a man apart, claiming two Olympic gold medals (1984 and 1992), one silver (1988), and one bronze (1996). Through their remarkable feats, Oerter, Harrison, Baumgartner, and so many others enhanced the precedent set by Thomas Burke, Ray Ewry, and others decades before. In so doing, they added luster to the Olympic renown of the New York Athletic Club, vindicating the faith and vision of the Club's founding members.

The 2012 Olympic Games in London saw New York Athletic Club athletes reach still higher. From a squad of fifty-five competitors, seventeen returned home with medals, these in fencing, water polo, rowing, judo, and track and field. In the most recent Games held in Rio de Janeiro in 2016, of the NYAC's sixty-eight representatives, twenty-one athletes won twenty-three medals. Twenty of those were gold. Notably, two NYAC athletes also competed in the Rio Paralympic Games, winning one gold medal.

In total, New York Athletic Club Olympians have won an astonishing 271 medals: 151 are gold, 54 are silver, and 66 are bronze. The commitment of the New York Athletic Club and its members to elite athletics and to the Olympic movement is a testimony to the vision of the Club's founders, who set out on this path of athletic excellence one hundred and fifty years ago. The successes of the NYAC's modern-day athletes are rooted in the commitment and steadfast dedication of those founders and those athletes who have gone before. Their legacy is one that not only endures but resonates around the world and in the highest echelons of international athletics.

# NYAC OLYMPIC MEDALISTS: 1896–2016

## 1896 – ATHENS

### GOLD MEDALIST
TRACK & FIELD
Thomas Burke, *100m, 400m*

## 1900 – PARIS

### GOLD MEDALISTS
TRACK & FIELD
Irving Baxter, *Running High Jump, Pole Vault*
Ray Ewry, *Standing High Jump, Standing Long Jump, Standing Triple Jump*
John Flanagan, *Hammer Throw*
Alvin Kraenzlein, *60m, 110m Hurdles, 200m Hurdles, Running Long Jump*
Maxwell Long, *400m*
George W. Orton, *2500m Steeplechase*
Richard Sheldon, *16lb Shot Put*

### SILVER MEDALISTS
SWIMMING
Otto Wahle, *1000m Freestyle, 200m Obstacle Race*

TRACK & FIELD
Irving Baxter, *Standing Triple Jump, Standing Long Jump, Standing High Jump*

### BRONZE MEDALISTS
TRACK & FIELD
Fay Moulton, *60m*
Lewis Sheldon, *Standing High Jump, Two Steps & Jump*
Richard Sheldon, *Discus Throw*

## 1904 – ST. LOUIS

### GOLD MEDALISTS
CYCLING
Marcus Hurley, *440yds, One-Third Mile, 880yds, One Mile*

SWIMMING
Charles Daniels, *4x50yds Relay, 220yds Freestyle, 440yds Freestyle*
Percy Dickey, *Diving - Plunge for Distance*
Leo "Budd" Goodwin, *4x50yds Relay*
Louis Handley, *4x50yds Relay*
Joseph Ruddy, *4x50yds Relay*

TRACK & FIELD
Ray Ewry, *Standing High Jump, Standing Long Jump, Standing Triple Jump*
John Flanagan, *Hammer Throw*
Harry Hillman, *400m, 200m Hurdles, 400m Hurdles*
Samuel Jones, *Running High Jump*
David Munson, *Four Mile Team Race*
Arthur Newton, *Four Mile Team Race*
Paul Pilgrim, *Four Mile Team Race*
George Underwood, *Four Mile Team Race*
Howard Valentine, *Four Mile Team Race*

WATER POLO
David Bratton
Leo "Budd" Goodwin
Louis Handley
David Hesser
Joseph Ruddy
James Steen
George Van Cleef

### SILVER MEDALISTS
SWIMMING
Edgar Adams, *Diving - Plunge for Distance*
Charles Daniels, *100yds Freestyle*
Francis Gailey, *220yds Freestyle*
H. R. Warren, *1 Mile Handicap*

TRACK & FIELD
John DeWitt, *Hammer Throw*
John Flanagan, *56lb Weight Throw*
David Munson, *One Mile Run*
George Underwood, *440yds Hurdles*
Howard Valentine, *800m Run*

### BRONZE MEDALISTS
CYCLING
Marcus Hurley, *Two Miles*

SWIMMING
Charles Daniels, *50yds Freestyle*
Leo "Budd" Goodwin, *Diving - Plunge for Distance*
Louis Handley, *880yds Freestyle*
Otto Wahle, *440yds Freestyle, One Mile Freestyle*

TRACK & FIELD
Lawrence Feuerbach, *16lb Shot Put*
James Mitchell, *Hammer Throw, 56lb Weight Throw*
Arthur Newton, *3000m Steeplechase, Marathon*
Robert Stangland, *Running Long Jump*

## 1906 – ATHENS
### (Inter-Calated Games)

### GOLD MEDALISTS
SWIMMING
Charles Daniels, *100m Freestyle*

TRACK & FIELD
Ray Ewry, *Standing High Jump, Standing Long Jump*
Paul Pilgrim, *400m, 800m*

### SILVER MEDALIST
TRACK & FIELD
Fay Moulton, *100m*

## 1908 – LONDON

### GOLD MEDALISTS
TENNIS
Jay Gould, *Jeu de Paume (Court Tennis)*

SWIMMING
Charles Daniels, *100m Freestyle*

TRACK & FIELD
Charles Bacon, *400m Hurdles*
Ray Ewry, *Standing High Jump, Standing Long Jump*
John Flanagan, *Hammer Throw*

### SILVER MEDALISTS
TRACK & FIELD
Harry Hillman, *400m Hurdles*
Matt McGrath, *Hammer Throw*
James Rector, *100m*

### BRONZE MEDALISTS
SWIMMING
Charles Daniels, *4x200m Freestyle Relay*

Leo "Budd" Goodwin, *4x200m Freestyle Relay*

TRACK & FIELD
John Eisele, *3000m Steeplechase*

## 1912 – STOCKHOLM

### GOLD MEDALISTS
SHOOTING
Charles Billings, *Trap (Clay Pigeon) Team*
Frank Hall, *Trap (Clay Pigeon) Team*
Alfred Lane, *Rapid Fire Pistol, Free Pistol, Military Revolver Team (50m)*
Daniel McMahon, *Trap (Clay Pigeon) Team*
Ralph Spotts, *Trap (Clay Pigeon) Team*

TRACK & FIELD
Platt Adams, *Standing High Jump*
Harry Babcock, *Pole Vault*
Pat McDonald, *Shot Put*
Matt McGrath, *Hammer Throw*
James "Ted" Meredith, *800m, 4x400m Relay*
Charles Reidpath, *400m, 4x400m Relay*

### SILVER MEDALISTS
TRACK & FIELD
Ben Adams, *Standing High Jump*
Platt Adams, *Standing Long Jump*
Pat McDonald, *Shot Put (Both Hands)*
James Wendell, *110m Hurdles*

### BRONZE MEDALISTS
TRACK & FIELD
Ben Adams, *Standing Long Jump*
Clarence Childs, *Hammer Throw*

## 1920 – ANTWERP

### GOLD MEDALISTS
TRACK & FIELD
Ivan Dresser, *3000m Team Race*
Richmond Landon, *High Jump*
Frank Loomis, *400m Hurdles*
Patrick McDonald, *56lb Weight Throw*
Loren Murchison, *4x100m Relay*
Jackson Scholz, *4x100m Relay*

SHOOTING
Karl Frederick, *Free Pistol*
Fred Plum, *Trap (Clay Pigeon)*
*Shooting Team*

WRESTLING
Eino Leino, *Freestyle Wrestling
(Middleweight)*

### SILVER MEDALISTS
TRACK & FIELD
Joseph Pearman, *10K Race Walk*

WRESTLING
Nathan Pendleton, *Freestyle
(Super Heavyweight)*

### BRONZE MEDALISTS
FENCING
Arthur Lyon, *Foil Team*

SHOOTING
Alfred Lane, *Free Pistol*

SWIMMING
Louis Balbach, *Diving - Springboard*

TRACK & FIELD
Fred Murray, *110m Hurdles*

## 1924 – PARIS

### GOLD MEDALISTS
SHOOTING
William Silkworth, *Trap (Clay Pigeon)*
*Shooting Team*

TENNIS
Francis Hunter, *Tennis (Doubles)*
Vincent Richards, *Tennis (Doubles),
Tennis (Singles)*

TRACK & FIELD
Allan Helffrich, *4x400m Relay*
Frank Hussey, *4x100m Relay*
Jackson Scholz, *200m*
William Stevenson, *4x400m Relay*

### SILVER MEDALISTS
TENNIS
Vincent Richards, *Tennis
(Mixed Doubles)*

TRACK & FIELD
Leroy Brown, *High Jump*
Matt McGrath, *Hammer Throw*
Jackson Scholz, *100m*

WRESTLING
Eino Leino, *Freestyle (Welterweight)*

### BRONZE MEDALIST
WATER POLO
Herbert Vollmer

## 1928 – AMSTERDAM

### GOLD MEDALISTS
TRACK & FIELD
Raymond Barbuti, *400m, 4x400m Relay*
Edward Hamm, *Long Jump*

WRESTLING
Osvald Kapp, *Freestyle Wrestling
(Lightweight)*

SWIMMING
George Kovac, *100m Backstroke,
4x200m Freestyle Relay*
Alberto Zorilla, *400m Freestyle*

### SILVER MEDALIST
TRACK & FIELD
Ben Hedges, *High Jump*

### BRONZE MEDALIST
TRACK & FIELD
John Collier, *100m Hurdles*

## 1932 – LOS ANGELES

### GOLD MEDALISTS
TRACK & FIELD
John Anderson, *Discus Throw*
Leo Sexton, *Shot Put*

### SILVER MEDALIST
TRACK & FIELD
Percy Beard, *110m Hurdles*

### BRONZE MEDALISTS
FENCING
Dernell Every, *Foil Team*
Frank Righeimer, *Foil Team, Epée Team*
Curtis Shears, *Epée Team*

MODERN PENTATHLON
Richard Mayo

TRACK & FIELD
Joseph McCluskey, *3000m Steeplechase*
Peter Zaremba, *Hammer Throw*

## 1936 – BERLIN

### SILVER MEDALIST
TRACK & FIELD
Eddie O'Brien, *4x400m Relay*

### BRONZE MEDALIST
ROWING
Daniel Barrow, *Single Scull*

## 1948 – LONDON

### GOLD MEDALIST
BASKETBALL
Ray Lumpp

### BRONZE MEDALISTS
FENCING
James Flynn, *Sabre Team*

TRACK & FIELD
James Fuchs, *Shot Put*

WRESTLING
Leland Merrill, *Freestyle (Welterweight)*

## 1952 – HELSINKI

### GOLD MEDALISTS
TRACK & FIELD
Horace Ashenfelter, *3000m Steeplechase*
Charles Moore, *400m Hurdles*
Lindy Remigino, *100m, 4x100m Relay*

### SILVER MEDALIST
TRACK & FIELD
Charles Moore, *4x400m Relay*

### BRONZE MEDALISTS
SWIMMING
Robert Clotworthy, *Diving - Springboard*

TRACK & FIELD
James Fuchs, *Shot Put*

## 1956 – MELBOURNE

### GOLD MEDALISTS
SWIMMING
Robert Clotworthy, *Diving - Springboard*

TRACK & FIELD
Thomas Courtney, *800m, 4x400m Relay*
Al Oerter, *Discus Throw*

## 1960 – ROME

### GOLD MEDALISTS
TRACK & FIELD
Al Oerter, *Discus Throw*

WRESTLING
Doug Blubaugh, *Freestyle (Welterweight)*

## 1964 – TOKYO

### GOLD MEDALIST
TRACK & FIELD
Al Oerter, *Discus Throw*

### SILVER MEDALIST
SWIMMING
Frank Gorman, *Diving - Springboard*

## 1968 – MEXICO CITY

### GOLD MEDALIST
TRACK & FIELD
Al Oerter, *Discus Throw*

### BRONZE MEDALIST
TRACK & FIELD
Tom Farrell, *800m*

## 1972 – MUNICH

### SILVER MEDALIST
TRACK & FIELD
Jay Silvester, *Discus Throw*

## 1976 – MONTREAL

### BRONZE MEDALS
GYMNASTICS
Peter Korman, *Floor Exercises*

WRESTLING
Stan Dziedzic, *Freestyle (Welterweight)*

## 1980 – MOSCOW

No US participation due to boycott

## 1984 – LOS ANGELES

### GOLD MEDALISTS
**Gymnastics**
Tim Daggett, *Team*

**Wrestling**
Bruce Baumgartner, *Freestyle (Super Heavyweight)*
Bobby Weaver, *Freestyle (Light Flyweight)*

### SILVER MEDALISTS
**Track & Field**
Mike Tully, *Pole Vault*

**Water Polo**
Gary Figueroa

### BRONZE MEDALISTS
**Gymnastics**
Tim Daggett, *Pommel Horse*

**Rowing**
Kevin Still, *Pair-Oared Shell with Coxswain*

## 1988 – SEOUL

### SILVER MEDALIST
**Wrestling**
Bruce Baumgartner, *Freestyle (Super Heavyweight)*

## 1992 – BARCELONA

### GOLD MEDALIST
**Wrestling**
Bruce Baumgartner, *Freestyle (Super Heavyweight)*

### SILVER MEDALIST
**Judo**
Jason Morris, *78kg*

### BRONZE MEDALIST
**Track & Field**
Joseph Greene, *Long Jump*

## 1996 – ATLANTA

### SILVER MEDALIST
**Track & Field**
Lance Deal, *Hammer Throw*

### BRONZE MEDALISTS
**Wrestling**
Bruce Baumgartner, *Freestyle (Super Heavyweight)*

**Judo**
Jimmy Pedro, *73kg*

## 2000 – SYDNEY

No NYAC medals

## 2004 – ATHENS

### GOLD MEDALISTS
**Rowing**
MEN
Christian Ahrens, *Eight*
Wyatt Allen, *Eight*
Peter Cipollone, *Eight*
Jason Read, *Eight*
Bryan Volpenhein, *Eight*

### SILVER MEDALIST
**Gymnastics**
Blaine Wilson, *Team*

### BRONZE MEDALISTS
**Judo**
Jimmy Pedro, *73kg*

**Water Polo**
WOMEN
Robin Beauregard
Natalie Golda
Heather Moody
Nicolle Payne

## 2008 – BEIJING

### GOLD MEDALIST
**Rowing**
WOMEN
Anna Mickelson-Cummins, *Eight*

### SILVER MEDALISTS
**Water Polo**
WOMEN
Natalie Golda
Heather Petri
Moriah Van Norman
Lauren Wenger
MEN
Tony Azevedo
Layne Beaubien
Rick Merlo
Merrill Moses
Jesse Smith
Adam Wright

### BRONZE MEDALISTS
**Judo**
WOMEN
Ronda Rousey, *70kg*

**Rowing**
MEN
Wyatt Allen, *Eight*
Beau Hoopman, *Eight*
Marcus McElhenney, *Eight*
Bryan Volpenhein, *Eight*

## 2012 – LONDON

### GOLD MEDALISTS
**Judo**
WOMEN
Kayla Harrison, *78kg*

**Rowing**
WOMEN
Erin Cafaro, *Eight*
Caryn Davies, *Eight*
Caroline Lind, *Eight*
Taylor Ritzel, *Eight*

**Swimming**
MEN
Tyler McGill, *4x100m Medley Relay*

**Water Polo**
WOMEN
Betsey Armstrong
Courtney Mathewson
Heather Petri
Kelly Rulon
Jessica Steffens
Lauren Wenger

### BRONZE MEDALISTS
**Track & Field**
MEN
Reese Hoffa, *Shot Put*

**Fencing**
WOMEN
Courtney Hurley, *Epée Team*
Kelley Hurley, *Epée Team*
Maya Lawrence, *Epée Team*

**Rowing**
WOMEN
Megan Kalmoe, *Quad Sculls*

## 2016 – RIO DE JANEIRO

### GOLD MEDALISTS
**Judo**
WOMEN
Kayla Harrison, *78kg*

**Rowing**
WOMEN
Eleanor Logan, *Eight*
Meghan Musnicki, *Eight*
Amanda Polk, *Eight*
Kerry Simmonds, *Eight*
Katelin Snyder, *Eight*

**Swimming**
WOMEN
Katie Meili, *4x100m Medley Relay*
MEN
Jimmy Feigen, *4x100m Freestyle Relay*
David Plummer, *4x100m Medley Relay*

**Track & Field**
WOMEN
Michelle Carter, *Shot Put*
Natasha Hastings, *4x400m Relay*

**Triathlon**
WOMEN
Gwen Jorgensen

**Water Polo**
WOMEN
K.K. Clark
Kami Craig
Kaleigh Gilchrist
Ashleigh Johnson
Courtney Mathewson
Kiley Neushul
Melissa Seidemann
Maggie Steffens

### SILVER MEDALIST
**Judo**
MEN
Travis Stevens, *81kg*

### BRONZE MEDALISTS
**Swimming**
MEN
David Plummer, *100m Backstroke*
WOMEN
Katie Meili, *100m Breaststroke*

One of the most iconic victories in the storied history of the Boston Marathon was that of NYAC member Meb Keflezighi, who claimed victory in 2014, one year after the Boston bombings.

# CHAPTER IV
# ATHLETICS

# GREAT THINGS

It is an honor and a pleasure to wear the winged foot logo of the New York Athletic Club. I make that statement speaking for more than just myself. The New York Athletic Club's support of our team handball squad has enabled my teammates and me to continue to compete in and to win many US national championships (seven since 2005) that would not otherwise have been possible for us. The generosity of the Club's membership, the support of the Board of Governors, the wise counsel of the Captain, Athletic Chairman, Athletic Director, and Athletic Committee—all of these have enabled us to continue our athletic careers and to pursue our dreams.

Similarly, the support of the NYAC has seen athletes of every level—from recreational runners to Olympic champions—reach heights that would otherwise have been beyond their reach. The evidence lies in the NYAC's catalog of Olympic, world, and national champions, a catalog that is unprecedented and impossible to match. To be part of that esteemed group, in the company of such great athletes, is humbling.

The NYAC's support of athletics at every level has created a culture in which we all strive to be "champions," to be extra prepared and to perform extra well in order to meet the expectations that come with wearing the winged foot. There is a sense of responsibility to maintain the standards set by the Club's great athletes who have gone before. By creating such wonderful athletic opportunities for its members, the New York Athletic Club has created an environment in which excellence can thrive and in which dreams may be fulfilled. Irrespective of age and ability, that is a rare and priceless gift to any athlete.

—*Thomas Fitzgerald, 1996 Olympian, Team Handball*

# ATHLETICS

Since before its formal inception, athletics has been at the core of the New York Athletic Club. The Club's three founders, William Curtis, Henry Buermeyer, and John Babcock, had been pursuing athletic excellence for many years prior to organizing the Club. It became their mission to bring amateur athletics to a larger group of people with a more formal structure and a governing code of rules. Prior to their innovations, athletics in the United States was in disarray, lacking standardized regulations and formalized means to measure results, weights, heights, and distances.

The vision and determination of Buermeyer, Babcock, and Curtis ensured that the promotion of athletics was—and is—always front and center for the New York Athletic Club. This has continued to be the focus throughout the years, just as it was during the early years as the Club was rising to become one of the preeminent organizations in the sporting world. As noted in the chapter "Olympic Games," the NYAC spends a considerable amount of time, effort, and resources in supporting its world-class athletes both during training and in their efforts to compete at the highest levels. But it also provides tremendous athletic opportunities and support for its members at every level.

One of the earliest recorded mission statements of the New York Athletic Club was "to promote manly sports." This, of course, evolved to include both men and women, and in almost every imaginable sporting category, from indoor sports to those played on a field, in the water, on a court, or on a track. Today, the NYAC is especially proud to support athletes competing in the Paralympic Games.

It need hardly be said that the athletic history of the New York Athletic Club is rich. Among its earliest distinctions, it hosted, in 1868, the country's first indoor track and field meet, this coming only a few months after the Club was formally organized. Notable enough in itself, this was also the first time that spiked shoes were used in the United States at a properly organized track event, and it was the first public appearance of a velocipede, or early bicycle. From its beginnings, the New

The Olympic Games are in the DNA of the New York Athletic Club, but athletic opportunities are available for members at every level, whether they are seeking the peaks of Mount Olympus or the peaks of that hill just up ahead.

NEW YORK ATHLETIC CLUB "HOCKEY TEAM" 1900-1901

J. A. FENWICK          E. J. GIANNINI          F. S. WONHAM

E. J. O'DONNELL          T. A. HOWARD, Captain          A. G. FRY          R. A. HUNT

M. HORNFECK          W. A. BELDEN

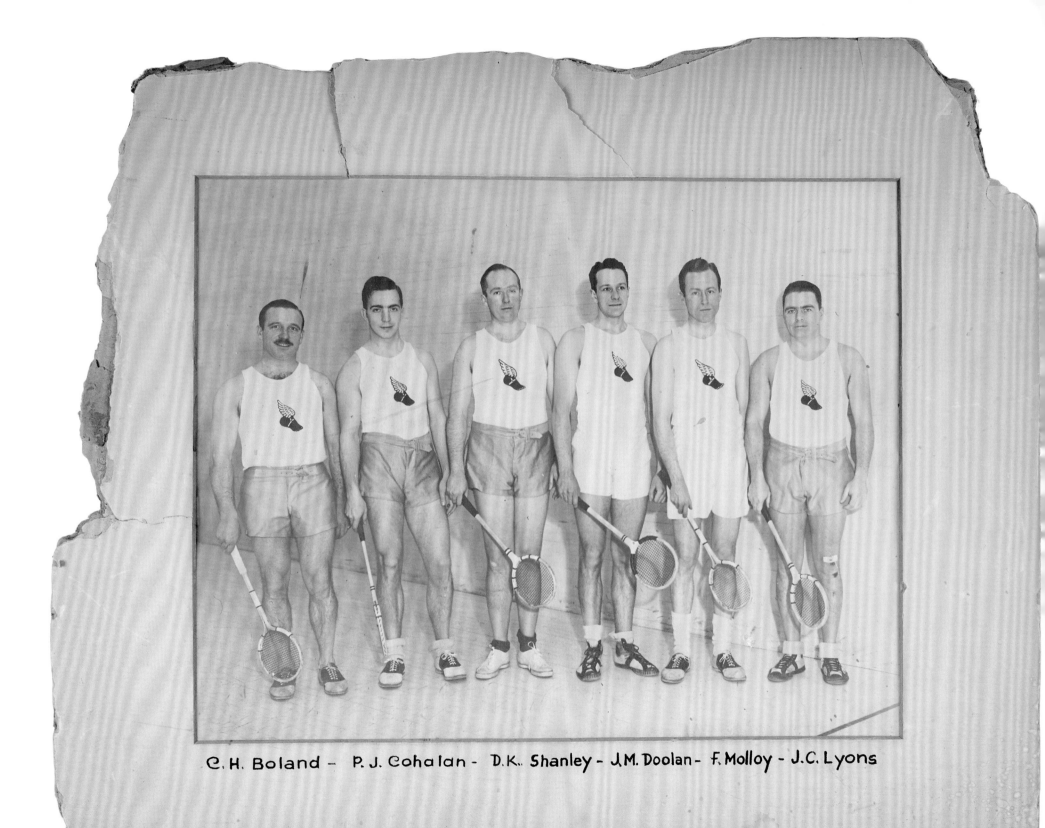

C. H. Boland - P. J. Cohalan - D. K. Shanley - J. M. Doolan - F. Molloy - J. C. Lyons

York Athletic Club was a pioneer in promoting athletics and sportsmanship. Its numerous innovations and advancements helped establish athletics on solid ground in the United States; its enduring commitment has proven a bulwark of amateur athletics for one hundred and fifty years.

T rack and field, swimming, and rowing were three of the primary sports in which members competed during the early days of the Club. The Elysian Fields in Hoboken, New Jersey, in 1870, and, starting in 1874, the Mott Haven Grounds along the Harlem River provided a great outdoor resource for competitions in these endeavors. The Club hosted the United States' first national track and field championships, held at Mott Haven in 1876 and, the following year, hosted the country's first national swimming championships, also at the Mott Haven facility.

With a strong framework in place for training and competition, the NYAC quickly became the leading athletic force in the United States. By default, the Club also became the unofficial governing body for its most prominent sports—something that was not planned. To help alleviate this great responsibility, members formed the National Association of Amateur Athletes of America (NAAAA), which included representatives from other athletic clubs. This group would evolve into the Amateur Athletic Union (AAU), which was founded at the New York Athletic Club in 1888.

The Club soon began to produce and attract some very talented and notable athletes. Bernie Wefers, who competed in the International Games of 1895, is considered to be one of the greatest sprinters who has ever lived. And, in the early 1890s, from humble beginnings the Club's "Chippie Crew" became a celebrated and accomplished group of rowers.

Charlie Moore reached Olympian heights at the Games of 1952, claiming the gold medal in the 400-meters hurdles. His path to glory wove through Travers Island, whence the Club sent him to live and train for a week in the build-up to those Games.

The roots of numerous sports sprang from the New York Athletic Club at the turn of the nineteenth century. Trapshooting became a popular activity at Travers Island and, in 1905, the NYAC began holding the national championships in that sport. Four Club members went on to compete in the world championships in 1933.

Hand tennis originated at the New York Athletic Club and remained an NYAC tradition, if not an anachronism, into the twenty-first century. It was first played at the Club in the late 1880s when Athletic Director Gene Giannini came up with the idea of stretching a rope across a court in the gymnasium, with each opponent using their hands to hit the ball back and forth. Members' access to tennis proper was enhanced when the Club purchased Travers Island in 1888 and tennis courts were built, spurring the popularity of that sport in New York and farther afield.

Fencing and baseball were introduced at the NYAC in the late 1800s and both quickly picked up momentum. Several New York Athletic Club members traveled to Paris in 1878 for an opportunity to learn fencing, returning to the Club to share the knowledge they had acquired with other members. The New York Athletic Club was among the first organizations to introduce that sport to the United States, and it remains among the Club's most successful athletic programs.

Boxing was a passion of Club founder Henry Buermeyer; he had fought in the ring while serving in the Union army. The sport became extremely popular, and the Club instigated the first national boxing championship in 1878, which was held at Madison Square Garden. Today, the NYAC maintains two boxing rings on the seventh floor of the City House and plays host to a major collegiate tournament and the New York City Golden Gloves event.

178

Initially, most athletes training at Travers Island were rowers, including the champion "Chippie Crew." This group began its competitive life as juniors in 1890, rowing for simple amusement. Seeing their first clumsy outing in an eight-man shell, a veteran oarsman reputedly remarked, "Who let those chippies out?" The name stuck. The Chippie Crew ended the 1890 season having won junior eight titles. In 1891, they won intermediate and senior eight titles and, in 1892, the national regatta held at Lake Saratoga in upstate New York. The Chippies are pictured training at Travers Island.

# · CHAMPIONS · OF · UNITED · STATES ·
## · AND ·
## · CANADA ·
## · 1929 – 1931 ·

# · WATER · POLO · TEAM ·

· JOE RUDDY COACH · — JOE FARLEY · — HALL VOLLMER · — TED CANN · — TOM MᶜCARTHY COACH ·
· LEO GEIBEL · — RAY RUDDY · — STEVE RUDDY JR. CAPTAIN · — JOHN CURREN · — BUD CATTUS ·

Benyon
(England)
3rd

Hurley
(U.S.)
1st

(Reid)
(England)
2nd

Crystal Palace
London
England
Sept. 1904.

ABOVE: The NYAC's judo program has produced legendary champions such as Jimmy Pedro (pictured top), Kayla Harrison, Travis Stevens, and Jason Morris. The Club also nurtures young talent, as evidenced by Morris's daughter, Randi—clearly a giant killer—pictured below. OPPOSITE: The gymnastics program, no longer in existence at the Club, nurtured talent such as Olympic gold medalist Tim Daggett.

The NYAC's track and field team competed at the National AAU Championships at the World's Fair in 1893; at the 1939 World's Fair, the NYAC flag was prominently displayed in the Court of Sports. These instances are illustrative of the enormous success that NYAC track and field athletes enjoyed during that era—and continue to enjoy at the highest levels to this day.

The Club's interest in wrestling started early, and the team grew under the direction of coach Hugh Leonard in the late 1800s. As a pioneer in this sport in the United States, the New York Athletic Club held the country's first national championships in 1879. Today, Club wrestlers compete at a multitude of levels including major international tournaments around the world.

During the months when the weather is amenable, yacht racing is a popular part of the sporting scene at Travers Island, while many members also participate at golfing events around the tristate area, including the annual NYAC Athlete's Fund Golf Tournament, held each August at the renowned Winged Foot Golf Club.

The Club expends tremendous resources in making athletic opportunities available to all of its members, and offers unwavering support to those who wish to train and compete at the highest levels; this support begins with the youngest of enthusiasts.

Founded in 1896, the same year as the inauguration of the Modern Olympic Games, the popular Saturday Morning Program for children of members offers instruction to young athletes in a wide array of sports including swimming, judo, track and field, water polo, basketball, and fencing. In the winter, the Program takes place at the City House; in the summer, it moves to Travers Island. The SMP, as it is universally dubbed, motivates children to get involved in athletics at a young age and maintains the Club's mission through the next generation of athletes. More than one Olympian has emerged from the SMP.

In more recent times, the NYAC has initiated a series of junior programs at both the City House and Travers Island, providing training in soccer, water polo, basketball, squash, tennis, sailing, swimming, lacrosse, and other sports. These programs, too, teach children the valuable lessons of sportsmanship and healthy competition.

The New York Athletic Club provides a tremendous infrastructure and an abundance of resources for athletes of all ages and abilities, regardless of whether their focus is pickup basketball or Olympic glory. Further complementing its mission, the Club established the Athlete's Fund, a registered charity that provides support for NYAC athletes training for the Olympic Games. The Fund also contributes money to a variety of fine causes including the Ronald McDonald House and numerous organizations that provide opportunities for inner-city children to take part in sports.

The vision of three sports enthusiasts in a New York City apartment in the 1860s has spawned an iconic institution in which, today, members may avail of the opportunity to take part in cycling, judo, water polo, track and field, tennis, swimming, rowing, boxing, rugby, wrestling, and many more sports—regardless of age, ability, or aspiration. While the Club's unwavering commitment to elite competition is evidenced by even a cursory glance into the Hall of Fame, the opportunities that exist for members of every age and ability are universally lauded as beyond compare.

The New York City Marathon is an annual highlight for NYAC members, be they elite competitors, recreational runners or sideline supporters. Gwen Jorgensen (opposite in red-striped shirt) contested the 2016 NYC Marathon less than three months after having won a triathlon gold medal at the Rio Olympic Games.

The NYAC Yacht Club is highly active at Travers Island, not to mention in the Long Island Sound and along the waters of the East Coast. Similarly, early most mornings the crew teams may be seen plying the local waters, their sights set on perpetuating the Club's rowing legacy.

Opportunities abound for participation in all manner of sports at the New York Athletic Club. From judo to skiing to swimming to cycling, the emphasis is on healthy enjoyment as much as it is on competition.

# CHAPTER V
# MEMBERSHIP

# A SPECIAL EXPERIENCE

Being a member of the NYAC is very special to me. I was first introduced to the Club and all it offers through my husband, now a forty-year member. When the opportunity for membership became available for women, I applied, and I am now a twenty-five-year member. On April 13, 2016, I was graciously inducted into the Quarter Century Club with Donna Hill, as the first female members, by QCC President Tom Quinn, with NYAC President Dominic Bruzzese in attendance.

The Club offers numerous activities both at the City House and Travers Island. The tennis, swimming, and dining facilities at Travers Island are a perfect summer respite. The City House has so many activities in which to participate; a favorite of mine has been the yoga class. Socially the dining facilities have been wonderful for a Sunday brunch, a Tap Room get-together, or a delicious dinner in the Main Dining Room. I attend many of the Club's special events—to name a few, the President's Ball, New Year's Eve, Mother's Day, Easter, and others. The Club is an important part of my social activities, which I enjoy with friends, old and new.

My professional career was in education as an elementary school teacher, in New York City. I also served as a teacher trainer, and Director of Retiree Programs for the United Federation of Teachers, with members and chapters across the country. I appreciate the work that the president, officers, and governors do in keeping the New York Athletic Club as the number one athletic club in the country, and I look forward to many more enjoyable years as an NYAC member.

*—Candy Cook, one of the NYAC's longest-serving female members*

# MEMBERSHIP

From its earliest days, the New York Athletic Club assumed the role of organizer, leader, and pioneer in amateur athletics in the United States. The Club led the way for the rest of the country by hosting the first of countless events, including inaugural national championships in boxing, wrestling, track and field, swimming, trapshooting, and rowing. In 1895, the New York Athletic hosted the International Games, a dual meet with the London Athletic Club and, at the time, a competition of global significance.

The Club's tradition of leading and organizing extends beyond sporting competition; that innovative spirit carries over to member functions and social events that are organized to celebrate NYAC athletic accomplishments, to immerse the full membership in those successes, and to enhance the sense of community across all Club members, be they Olympic gold medalists, weekend warriors, or fans on the couch. These events often play an essential role in maintaining interest in health, fitness, and competition and in continuing the NYAC's founding mandate.

It is because of the dedication and commitment of its members that the New York Athletic Club has been able to remain not only relevant, but also one of the most dominant and well-respected forces in the now global world of athletics throughout the past one hundred and fifty years. The New York Athletic Club has endured a depression, a recession, two world wars, and countless other challenges that have strained and sometimes shuttered many other private clubs and institutions.

Of course, the mandate of the New York Athletic Club is to promote athletics, but it is the membership that perpetuates that mission for each generation to enjoy. The Club provides a wonderfully unique environment and resources for members of all ages and abilities in which they can train, compete, and socialize; the resulting energy and vibrancy are evident

For members of the New York Athletic Club, a year-round schedule of events, dinners, and activities ensures that there is something to appeal to every taste. Further, the Club's more than forty Intra Clubs are the lifeblood of the NYAC, offering something for everybody, regardless of whether your passion is backgammon or billiards, ballroom dancing or theater.

**1895**

FIFTY-FOURTH GAMES

w York Athletic Club,

TRAVERS ISLAND,
Pelham Manor, N. Y

TURDAY, JUNE 15th, 1895,
Beginning at 2 P. M.

en to all Amateurs.
of the Amateur Athletic Union and League of American
men to govern all competitions. Bicycle races sanctioned
irman Gideon.

OSITIVELY NO POSTPONEMENT.

HANDICAP EVENTS:

ARD RUN. 1 MILE WALK.
ARD RUN. THROWING 16 LB. HAMMER.
ARD RUN 15 Yards Limit POLE VAULT.
ARD RUN. 25 Yards Limit 2 MILE BICYCLE.
1 MILE RUN. 60 Yards Limit.

SCRATCH EVENTS:

ARD HURDLE RACE. 1 MILE BICYCLE.
ARD HURDLE RACE. PUTTING 16 LB. SHOT
ING BROAD JUMP. THROWING 56 LB. WEIGHT
RUNNING HIGH JUMP.
For men who have never jumped 6 Feet.

sion to Club Grounds by Invitation only.
Train to reach Grounds before Games.
Medal to First, Silver to Second and Bronze to Third in
nt.

ght to reject or strike out any entry is reserved.
ce Fee, $1.00 per man for each event.

es close Wednesday, June 5th, With

JOHN C. GULICK,

55th St., N. Y. City. Secretary.

**1868**                                              **1895**

FIFTY-FOURTH GAMES

New York Athletic Club,

TRAVERS ISLAND,
Pelham Manor, N. Y

SATURDAY, JUNE 15th, 1895,
Beginning at 2 P. M.

Open to all Amateurs.
Rules of the Amateur Athletic Union and League of American
Wheelmen to govern all competitions. Bicycle races sanctioned
by Chairman Gideon.

POSITIVELY NO POSTPONEMENT.

HANDICAP EVENTS:

100 YARD RUN. 1 MILE WALK.
220 YARD RUN. THROWING 16 LB. HAMMER.
440 YARD RUN 15 Yards Limit POLE VAULT.
880 YARD RUN. 25 Yards Limit 2 MILE BICYCLE.
1 MILE RUN. 60 Yards Limit.

SCRATCH EVENTS:

120 YARD HURDLE RACE. 1 MILE BICYCLE.
220 YARD HURDLE RACE. PUTTING 16 LB. SHOT
RUNNING BROAD JUMP. THROWING 56 LB. WEIGHT
RUNNING HIGH JUMP.
For men who have never jumped 6 Feet.

Admission to Club Grounds by Invitation only.
Special Train to reach Grounds before Games.
Gold Medal to First, Silver to Second and Bronze to Third in
each event

The right to reject or strike out any entry is reserved.
Entrance Fee, $1.00 per man for each event.

Entries close Wednesday, June 5th, With

JOHN C. GULICK,

104 W. 55th St., N. Y. City. Secretary.

throughout the City House and Travers Island. The common mission is to promote athletics; the consequences are tangible, in the trophies in the Hall of Fame, in the countless events and activities that personify the Club, and in the vitality that imbues its members.

Many of the NYAC's most popular events are longstanding traditions that were established decades ago, sometimes during much harder times such as war or the Depression. The Board of Governors and the Club's various committees have always worked tirelessly to organize a broad spectrum of special events, dinners, programs, and awards ceremonies in order to encourage members to become involved and help support the Club's mission of promoting athletics.

In the early 1900s, Colonel Robert Thompson, president of the American Olympic Committee and a member of the International Olympic Committee, would organize large dinners at the Club to encourage members to financially support athletics and the NYAC's participation in the Olympic Games. In doing this, he was successful in nurturing the membership's interest in furthering the Club's mission, as well as ensuring the success of the young and fragile Olympic movement.

During the Great Depression and in the years that followed, the NYAC organized numerous events to boost members' spirits and keep the mission of athletics alive and well. Theater nights and other themed evenings were introduced to help integrate the Club into members' lives. Programs were also developed for veterans returning from war and who were having a challenging time finding employment. The New York Athletic Club founded its own post of the American Legion in 1919; Post 754 remains highly active to this day.

In 1896, the Club initiated the Saturday Morning Program to introduce members' children to athletics at an early age. The SMP—originally known as the Saturday Morning Boys program—continues today and is one of the Club's most

Athletics at all levels has always been at the heart of the New York Athletic Club, be it recreational outings or elite competitions such as the NYAC Games (shown here with the legendary Glenn Cunningham ready to run an exhibition race in the "Night of Mile Legends" in 1962), the Millrose Games, or the Olympic Games.

Through the decades, the NYAC's support of athletics has gone hand in hand with an emphasis on camaraderie, building a unique rapport between the NYAC's top class athletes and its membership base. Special events, outings and gala occasions have always supported that sentiment. LEFT: The US Olympic team bound for Stockholm in 1912, including many NYAC members, received a rousing send-off at New York harbor. ABOVE: At the Club, events such as the All Sports Dinner, the President's Ball and the Winged Foot Awards have all embraced the over-arching philosophy of reaching for excellence in all endeavors, athletic and otherwise.

Artifacts illustrating the NYAC's remarkable history may be found in countless nooks around the City House and Travers Island. Both facilities constitute a unique trove of antiquities.

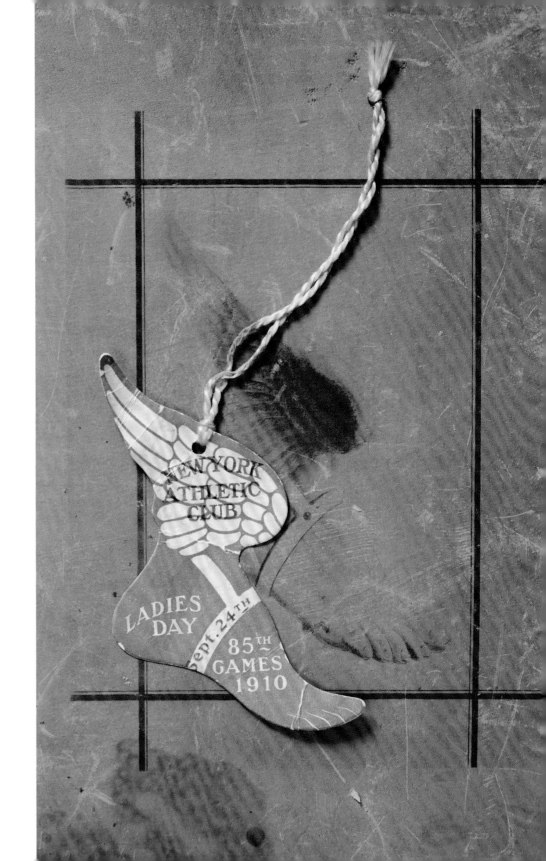

Athletics is the heart of the Club, but camaraderie and enjoyment are similarly fundamental. ABOVE: Pictured at the June 9, 1940, Spring Games at Travers Island are past NYAC President William Dalton, Chairman of Athletics John Storm, and Athletic Director Paul Pilgrim, a 1906 Olympic champion at 400 meters and 800 meters.

popular programs. It is not uncommon to see more than one hundred children participating in different athletic events on any given Saturday at the City House during the winter or at Travers Island in the summer.

The All Sports Dinner, which started in 1932, is a large-scale gala that honors the outstanding achievements of the Club's athletes throughout the year. Not only is this event well attended, with typically over six hundred guests, but there is also a celebrity guest speaker, plus presentations and videos highlighting the accomplishments of the New York Athletic Club's elite athletes. This event is the perfect reminder of the things for which the Club stands and the athletic excellence that it fosters.

The New York Athletic Club has over forty Intra Clubs—clubs within the Club. These specialized groups bring together members with common interests and goals. They include boxing, backgammon, chess, soccer, scuba diving, running, fine arts, ballroom dancing, and countless others. The Quarter Century Club is an Intra Club of particular note. It is open to individuals who have been members of the New York Athletic Club for twenty-five years or longer. The QCC hosts a monthly gathering, plus an annual banquet at which the NYAC's Member of the Year and Athlete of the Year are recognized.

The New York Athletic Club is a remarkable institution with worldwide prominence due to the enduring commitment of its members to the goals put in place by its founders one hundred and fifty years ago. A healthful lifestyle underpinned by a striving for excellence—the Club has been successful in adhering to this tradition for over one hundred and fifty years. In the years to come, that adherence will remain steadfast, as will the pride that the NYAC's members take in perpetuating their club as a singular organization on the stage of global athletics.

The Fashion Show at Travers Island is as popular in 2018 as it has ever been.

The plaque over the mantel in the Travers Island Club House reads, "In Memoriam James Henry Haslin, Governor of the Club for fifteen years and President 1909 – 1910. It was greatly due to his efforts that this house was built." OPPOSITE: Both Travers Island and the City House are alive with activities and events for members, year round. Headgear is usually not required.

TESTIMONIAL BEEFSTEAK DINNER
TENDERED BY
ARTHUR M°ALEENAN (CAPTAIN)
TO THE
ATHLETES OF THE NEW YORK
ATHLETIC CLUB WHO SCORED
PLACES IN CHAMPIONSHIPS
DURING THE YEARS 1920,
1921 AND 1922.
N.Y.A.C.        APRIL 20th 1922.

The Hall of Fame Banquet, the Winged Foot Awards Dinner, the President's Ball, the All Sports Dinner, the Quarter Century Club Banquet—these, and many more, events embrace the NYAC's history and acknowledge its athletic successes while perpetuating the atmosphere of camaraderie for which the Club has long been renowned.

# NYAC 150TH ANNIVERSARY BENEFACTORS

GOLD LEVEL
Peter Abate
Hania Abrous-McCarthy
Alex Afkhami
Pavlos M. Alexandrakis
Stephanos Alexiou
Andrew C. Ambruoso
Anonymous
Art Antin
Richard J. "RJ" Bannister, Jr.
Alexandra Benenson
Courtney Hope Benenson
Harvey L. and Sandra C. Benenson
Ajay Bhumitra
Steven H. Biondolillo
Elizabeth Boehmler
Stefan R. Bothe
William D. Brewer
Dominic Bruzzese
Donald W. Burkett
Edward J. Caffrey
James D. Cameron
Michael Carty
Petey Caulo
Peter R. Cella
Joseph G. Cesare, Jr.
Mark E. Chiaviello
Richard A. Cini, Sr.
Curt and Madalena Clausen
Steven Clausen
William C. Close
William Coldrick
CJ Coleman
Robert B. Collins
John Concannon
Raymond F. Condon
Candy Cook
Ronald Cook
P. Christopher Cotronei
James Joseph Cotter, Sr.*

Christopher Croft
Matthew F. Culen
Mario J. D'Aiuto* and
    Samiha Koura D'Aiuto
Erickson Davis
J. Stewart Deindorfer
John Thomas Delaney
Thomas F. Delaney
Frank DelPonte
Joseph A. Del Vecchio
Joseph V. Di Mauro
Anthony J. Di Santo
Mark C. DiMilia
Raymond L. Dudzinski
John Duggan
Patrick and Amy Durkan
Thomas E. Durkin III
Patrick J. Egan
David E. Eifrig, Jr.
Peter H. Elson
Diana M. Elton and
    Robert J. Radway
John Erickson
Ricardo J. Escudero
The Fajardo Family
John Nicholas Favale
Robert B. Feduniak
William Ferguson and
    Christine Ferguson
Telesforo Fernandez, Jr.
Daniel H. Fitzgerald
Patrick Flatley
Lawrence and Megan Foley
David A. Foxen
William Samuel Frank
Dempsey L. and Bette S. Gable
Mark W. Gaffney
Victor T. Gainor III
Ciro Jerry Galano
Anna Gary

Jacqueline B. Gaul
John P. Gaul
Kevin G. Geiger
Linda and Jack Gill
Louis Gioia
Christopher P. Golden
William E. W. Gowen
Michael Graff
Frank J. Guarini
John F. Gunn
Lily Han
Patrycia (Pat) Harbison
William B. Harford, Jr.
Christopher Haschek
The Haskins Family
Brian Healy
Billy Heinzerling
John J. Hennessy
James D. Herschlein
Steven R. Hirsch
Mike Hoover
Marc T. Hudak
Lyn and Ralph Ianuzzi
Joseph P. Iodice
Lara and Sam Jacob
Vincent W. Ji
Stephen Juliano
Peter A. Junge
Eckart Kade
Joseph Keane*
Melissa Keene
Regina and Bill Keller
Brian G. Kelly
Mark S. Kiely
Gregory Kincheloe
Burton Kossoff*
Chris Kovacs
Peter and Brett Larkin
Luke P. La Valle, Jr.
John Lee

Richard J. Lindquist
Lawrence LoIacono
Marie Therese Luzine-Baker
Thomas C., Caitlin, Megan and
    Thomas M. Lynch
Ronald F. MacDonald
Kerrie D. MacPherson
Michael J. Maimone
Jack Makoujy
Timothy and Noreen Marsek
Peter F. Matthews*
Daniel Mazzella
Holt McCallany
Brian J. McCarthy
Joseph McCarthy
Neil M. McCarthy
John J. McDermott
Michael Sean McGeary
Sean Joseph McLaughlin
Daniel B. McManus
John Kevin Medica
John Joseph Meglio
Charles Mele
Daniel Molino
Michael J. Monahan
David and Nanjoo Moore
James J. Moore
Daniel J. More
Gary Morgan
Eric L. Munson
Karol Louise Murov
Joseph M. Murphy
Katrina Nath
John W. Neary
S. Colin Neill
Gregory Mark Nespole
Arno P. Niemand
John Nonna
Michael and Donna Noone
    and Family

Cardinal Edwin O'Brien
James W. and Kathleen O'Brien
Jonathan O'Brien
James O'Connor
William J. O'Hagan
Anthony Orlando
Ronald D. Ormand
Louis Johannes Pappas
Joseph and Eileen Pash
Laurence Pels
Nelson Peltz
Barnet Phillips IV
Dean J. Poll
Robert J. Ponzini
William C. Powers
E. Miles Prentice III
Thomas D. Quinn
James B. Rafferty
Naresh and Sneha Rao and Family
Lawrence Rawson
Luis Roberto Rey G.
Mark S. Reilly
Jack Ribeiro
Richard V. Robilotti
Frank and May Rocco
Robin Roshkind
Thomas Ryan
David Sadroff
David J. Samuel
Anurag Sanyal
The Scarangella Family
Richard M. Scarlata
Richard R. Schilling III
Andrew Charles Schirrmeister III
Mark Settembre
Dave J. Shakespeare
Vance P. Shaw
M. David Sherrill
Barbara Siegler
The Signorile Family

Thomas L. Smario
Grant Smith
Stephen C. Smith
James K. Smyth
Cindy Spera
J. Gary Stanco
Vincent T. Striano
Casey P. Sullivan
William T. Sullivan
Robert M. Tamiso
Richard G. Tashjian
James W. Taylor
George J. Todd
Peter Carson Trent
Andrew Charles Tsunis
William J. Tully*
Joseph Urbinati, Sr.
Joseph Urbinati, Jr.
Joseph Urbinati III
Michele Beverly Urbinati
Charles Vadala
Robert Valdes-Rodriguez
Vincent and Cathleen Ventura
Michael J. Volpe
Leslie Wade
Leon Wagner
John J. Walsh
Stephen L. Weiner
Jonathan and Lisa Wells
Kevin D. White
Brent and Mari Willey
David J. Wolf
Richard Yau
Kenneth Q. Yip
Victor A. Zollo, Jr.

## SILVER LEVEL

James J. Bauman
Mimi Bean
Jonathan Biele
Michael Blasi
Kyle Newman Bohan
Amelia and Edward J. Bowes
Marsha W. Bramowitz
Thomas A. Burger, Jr.
Josephine and Frank J.* Cassata
Anthony J. Cassino
Mark and Judi Chiusano
George H. Connerat, Jr.
Marcia Eileen Connolly
Stephen J. Cornwall
Robert A. Cowie
Richard J. Daileader
J. Richard deBart, Jr.
Timothy and Joan Delaney
John P. and Andrew F.J.
    Della Ratta
Alec Harry Diacou
James Vincent Dillon, Jr.
James P. Farley*
Egidio A. Farone
Christian M. Fisch
Ronald A. Fisher
Richard M. Frome
Stephen E. Gallucci
John Gardiner
David A. Gellman
Matthew Q. Giffuni
Thomas Glanfield
Bruce L. Goodman
Thomas K. Guba
Cory S. Gunderson
Paul Guyet
James E. Helmus
John D. Herrick
Aaron Iskowitz

Jeffrey Jones
Thomas W. Keaveney
Alfred F. Kelly, Jr.
Michael Kennedy*
Robert E. Kennedy
Sean T. Kilduff
Jeremiah William Kohler
Torodd Kummen
David Landman
Stephen Lovelette
Thomas P. Maginnis
Mark Maher
William C. Mattison, Jr.
James E. Mercante
Robert Milam
Stephen Munk
Maria Nardone
Kenneth R. Nolan
Charles John O'Byrne
Richard L. O'Hara
Stuart E. Patchen
Gautam G. Patwa
W. Frank Phillips
Vincent and JoMarie Pica
Arun K. Prasad
Michael T. Prousis
William Rahal
Maureen C. Regan
Michael K. Reidy
Bernard Robinson
Paul and Michele Romanello
Christina Rose and Family
Peter E. Scales
Peter J. Schmole
Frank Schwitter
Joseph J. Seymour
W. Gregg Slager
Brayton "Bray" Smith
Christian Stanco
Tad Waldbauer

Jerry Whipple
Leonard A. Wilf
Brian J. Woods
Madeleine Zuccala

## BRONZE LEVEL

Jennifer Abate
Humayun Agha
Ashley Hearst Agron
John B. Amendola
George A. Ashur
Barbara Atkins
James Barnes
Eugene* and Deidre Bay
Jay Bikofsky
John Wesley Blackwell
Andrew F. Blumenthal
Edward T. Boehlke
Kevin G. Boll
Joe Borini
Stephen F. Bornet, Sr.
Cara Boyce
Mark G. Brennan
Ronald J. Brien
Joyce Brody-Skodnek
Cirino M. Bruno
Christopher J. Byrne
Christopher T. Byrne
Mary E. Byrne
Susan Camus
Brenna C. Carlin
Jack L. Carlson
Andrew Carr
Liam J. and Katharine T.
    Carroll and Family
Thomas G. Cascione
Alfred Cavallaro
Gerard J. Chambers
Tania Chebli
Richard A. Cini, Jr.

William P. Cleary
Catherine, Kieran and
    Charlotte Coffey
Thomas F. Colasuonno
Michelle Copeland
Peter P. Corritori, Jr.
Leonard W. Cox
Peter C. Coxhead
Jerry L. Crispino and Family
David Crotty
Michael J. Curcio
Alain C. Daguillard
Richard W. Daidone
Gabriel Damascus
Peter Noble Darrow
Michael H. Davis
William A. DeSanto
David T. DeStefano
Peter M. DiCristofaro
Matthew and Kathleen Digan
Stafford Dobbin
John P. Docherty
Earl Donaldson
Thorne Donnelley
Mary Claire Dragoni
Dana E. Drury
James T. Dwyer III*
David Eber
Richard D. Fairman
Oksana Farber
Nadja Fidelia
Scott Flynn
Daniel Foxx
David Freylikhman
John F. Galbraith
Francis D. Gannon
Craig Gilbert
Marc Stuart Goldberg
Maura Gorman
Andrew Grabis

Michael J. Gregg
Robert Guglielmo
Rich Gumersell
R. Tomas Hannell
J. Nelson Happy
Daniel C. Harkins
Fred C. Hart
Brian J. Hecker
Jeffrey Heidelberger
Alex R. Helfand
James D. Henderson, Jr.
Peter Y. Hess
James E. Hillman
Donald W. Hinrichs, Jr.
Frank G. Hollander
G. Patrick Hunter III
Peter L. Jensen
Jorge R. Jiménez
John E. Jureller, Jr.
Diana Keenan
William T. Kennedy
Anderson Kenny
Kerry B. Kenny
Robert and Betty Kloepfer
Michael P. Koribanics
Anton F. Kreuzer
Paul Kuppich, Jr.
Joseph J. Labriola, Jr.
Andrew Lake
The Lauretani Family
George Lefkovits
Catherine Lenihan
Joseph C. Lentini, Jr.
Istvan Leovits
Par Lindstrom
Joseph Luchi
Kellie Lynch
Joseph Macedo
Gregory P. Maloof
Robert and Colleen Manfred
Jeffrey Alton Marcks
Richard H. Martin
Michael L. Martinez
Joseph and Yeila Martinous

Mario R. Masrieh
Joseph A. Mazzella
Tom McGee
Maurice McKenzie
Robert J. Menegaz
Felicia M. Messina
Frank "Dusty" Mormando
James Morris
Anthony R. Moscato
Paul R. Mrockowski
Esther Muller
Paul D. Muller
Canon Andrew J. W. Mullins
William Hugh Murray
K. Richard B. Niehoff
Xavier Noel
Astrid Norman
Thor O'Connell
Brian O'Connor
James Oestreich
Richard L. O'Hara, Jr.
Richard Pacheco
Robert and Francine Paino
Michael Pellegrino
James S. Peters
Marinos A. Petratos
Dennis McShane Potts
Jack Powers
David Matthew Rader
Ralph A. Ranghelli
Cassandra Ranghelli-Postighone
Caroline A. Raynis
Kirk and Susan Reische
Thomas Rogers
Richard B. Romney
Bob and Carol Rosiek
Anthony P. Salvatore
Melissa H. Sama
George W. Sanborn
Thomas D. Sanford
Benjamin A. Sarly
Frederick Sawabini
William and Catherine Scarpa, Jr.
Robert Morse Schroder*

Arthur Lott Scinta
Robert H. Shannon
Christina Sheng
Nathan Royce Silverstein
Lawrence I. Singer
Roberto Sisti
Craig J. Smith
Jeffrey A. and Pamela J. Smith
Leon H. Smith III
John M. Spiegel
Barbara and Jordan Sprechman
Timothy Gilbert Starr
George F. Staudter
Russell W. Steenberg
Jennifer Stewart
Joan K. Stout
Peter Sullivan
Michael G. Suscavage
Zarko Svatovic
Masahiro Takeda
Nicholas Taro
Nicola Tegoni
Christopher M. Tierney
Thomas V. Tinsley, Jr.
Michael J. Tricarico
Craig Vaream
Frank Vasti
John B. Vrabel
Keith H. Walker
Eva Marie Ward and
    Thomas J.* Ward
John J. Welde
Ellis Wells
Edward J. Winrow
Paul E. Wintrich
Henry F. White, Jr.
Paul P.* and Ruth F. Woolard
Natalie Wood
Dennis P. Yeskey
Nicholas E. Younker, Jr.

*Deceased

# NYAC PRESIDENTS

1868: J. Edward Russell
1869–1872: William E. Van Wyck
1873: George Moore Smith
1874–1875: D. M. Knowlton
1876: W. E. Sinclair
1877: W. K. Collins
1878: F. L. Haynes
1879: C. H. Pierce
1880–1881: William B. Curtis
1882–1887: William R. Travers
1888: A. V. deGoicouria
1889: Jennings S. Cox
1890: Walter S. Schuyler
1891: Abraham G. Mills
1892, 1894: Bartow S. Weeks
1893: August Belmont
1895–1898: James Whitely
1899: Thomas L. Watson
1900–1906: John R. VanWormer
1907–1908: George W. Kulke
1909–1910: James H. Haslin
1911–1912: Robert M. Thompson
1913–1915: William H. Page
1916–1919: Dr. Graeme M. Hammond
1920: George J. Corbett
1921: William MacMaster Mills
1922–1923: Frank Loughman
1924–1925: Arthur W. Teele
1926–1932: Major William Kennelly
1933–1936: William A. Dalton
1937–1940: Orie R. Kelly
1941–1942: Henry W. Ryan
1943–1944: Gilbert B. J. Frawley
1945: Lee S. Buckingham
1946–1948: Frank A. Sieverman
1949: James A. Norton
1949: Theodore J. Van Twisk
1950–1952: Harry L. Lindquist
1953–1955: John A. McNulty
1956–1958: Julien J. Soubiran

1959–1961: Joseph J. Lordi
1962–1963: James J. Wilson
1964–1966: Jerome F. Healy, Jr
1967–1969: W. Thomas Hoyt
1970–1972: William A. Rose
1973–1975: Richard E. Long
1976–1978: William H. McCarthy
1979–1981: Joseph P. Ingrassia
1982–1984: William P. Farrell
1985–1987: John J. McDermott
1988–1990: Wallace L. Beneville
1991–1993: John A. Johnson
1994–1996: Robert J. Cullum
1997–1999: James W. O'Brien
2000–2002: Alfred H. Green
2003–2005: John W. Neary
2006–2008: Valentine J. Taubner, Jr.
2009–2010: Robert F. Geary
2011–2013: S. Colin Neill
2014–2016: Dominic Bruzzese
2017–    James B. Rafferty

# THE
## NEW YORK ATHLETIC

## CLUB

Hereby Deeply Expresses Its Appreciation To

# GEORGE V. McLAUGHLIN

Governor 1952

Who as a Clubmember and as an Officer has contributed so much on behalf of the Club.

*President*

# ACKNOWLEDGMENTS

Many people were responsible for the production of this book, but particular gratitude must be extended to NYAC archivists Thomas Quinn and Mark Gaffney whose trojan work and dedication to the project were instrumental in bringing it to so successful a conclusion. Special thanks must also go to Charles Miers and James Muschett of Rizzoli USA, as it must to the members of the 150th Anniversary Committee: Chairman Colin Neill, NYAC Captain Thomas Lynch, Christopher Golden, Courtney Benenson, Peter Corritori, Patrick Egan, Mike Monahan, Anthony Orlando, Cindy Spera, Robert Valdes-Rodriguez and Jonathan Wells. The steadfast support of the NYAC Board of Governors, headed by President James Rafferty and Vice President Regina Conroy-Keller, was essential to the success of this considerable undertaking. Never to be overlooked are the contributions of all Club members through the years, but most particularly those of John Babcock, Henry E. Buermeyer and William Curtis, the Club's visionary founders, who, 150 years ago, set in motion a course of events that would enable the NYAC and its athletes to scale heights unimaginable.